To my lord, Jesus Christ, thank you for helping me find my way. To Alicia, Zack, and Kaleb, thank you for your love and support of my many academic endeavors.

Alan

Contents

JUMP*METRICS*

Alan Tyson
Ben Cook

HUMAN KINETICS

Library of Congress Cataloging-in-Publication Data

Tyson, Alan, 1968-
    Jumpmetrics / Alan Tyson, Ben Cook.
        p. cm.
    ISBN: 0-7360-4838-3 (Softcover)
    1. Jumping. 2. Exercise. 3. Physical fitness. I. Cook, Ben T. (Ben
Trelowe) II. Title.
    GV529.T96 2005
    796.4'32--dc22

                                                    200407255

ISBN: 0-7360-4838-3

Acquisitions Editor: Ed McNeely
Managing Editor: Melinda Graham
Assistant Editor: Scott Hawkins
Copyeditor: Pat Connolly
Proofreader: Kim Thoren
Graphic Designer: Robert Reuther
Graphic Artist: Francine Hamerski
Photo Manager: Dan Wendt
Cover Designer: Keith Blomberg
Photographer (cover): Dan Wendt
Photographer (interior): Kelly Huff, unless otherwise noted
Art Manager: Kareema McLendon
Illustrators: Kristine Mount and Mic Greenberg
Artist: Kareema McLendon
Printer: United Graphics

Human Kinetics books are available at special discounts for bulk purchase. Special editions or book excerpts can also be created to specification. For details, contact the Special Sales Manager at Human Kinetics.

Printed in the United States of America   10 9 8 7 6 5 4 3 2 1

Human Kinetics
Web site: www.HumanKinetics.com

United States: Human Kinetics
P.O. Box 5076
Champaign, IL 61825-5076
800-747-4457
e-mail: humank@hkusa.com

Canada: Human Kinetics
475 Devonshire Road Unit 100
Windsor, ON N8Y 2L5
800-465-7301 (in Canada only)
e-mail: orders@hkcanada.com

Europe: Human Kinetics
107 Bradford Road
Stanningley
Leeds LS28 6AT, United Kingdom
+44 (0) 113 255 5665
e-mail: hk@hkeurope.com

Australia: Human Kinetics
57A Price Avenue
Lower Mitcham, South Australia 5062
08 8277 1555
e-mail: liaw@hkaustralia.com

New Zealand: Human Kinetics
Division of Sports Distributors NZ Ltd.
P.O. Box 300 226 Albany
North Shore City
Auckland
0064 9 448 1207
e-mail: blairc@hknewz.com

Drill Finder

Introduction

More than 60,000 high school and college athletes will injure their knees this year. Will you be a member of that unlucky club? Sue Bird, Wesley Walls, Rebecca Lobo, and Jamal Anderson are former members. All of these athletes were having successful careers, but tearing their anterior cruciate ligament (ACL) slowed their progress. Athletes are currently facing a crisis. Year-round training programs are making athletes stronger, faster, and bigger, yet they are still being injured at an alarming rate. Females are two to six times more likely to suffer a serious knee injury than their male counterparts. Over the last 15 years, ankle sprains for women have decreased by 86 percent, while knee ligament injuries have increased by 172 percent[1] (Lobo 2000). Solving the problems with the knee ultimately depends on strength and kinesthetic awareness, and many athletes (especially females) are inherently deficient in both areas.

Like most athletes, you may feel that you have great body control. But when you squat or leg press, do your knees come inward as you push the weight up or do your heels leave the floor? Can you squat on one leg and keep your knee from going out over your toes? Can you stand on one foot and slowly kick one leg out to the side to form a perfect inverted L between your supporting and kicking leg? Or is your hip too weak to hold your leg high enough? If you find any of these simple tasks difficult, you may be losing critical power output that could help you jump higher and run faster, but more important, you may be setting yourself up for injury. We designed the Jumpmetrics sports performance plan to teach athletes and coaches how to evaluate current abilities in areas that are vital to performance and safety and to teach them how to address weaknesses in these areas. Whether you are a player or a coach, you can use this book to learn exercises that every athlete should be performing. In addition, in chapter 6 we present a 20-minute warm-up that has been shown to improve performance and decrease the rate of injury among athletes. We also illustrate a 6-week training program that when performed correctly and with attention to detail will help athletes improve their first-step explosion, leaping ability, and overall quickness. This comprehensive program will make athletes better and allow them to compete at their highest level.

The Jumpmetrics program is divided into easily understandable parts so that athletes and coaches at all levels can implement the program. Each variable of the training takes into consideration that today's athlete must be trained differently to improve performance and decrease the chance of knee injuries. What do we mean by different? We feel that more emphasis should be placed on body control, balance exercises, and hip strengthening. These

---

[1] Lobo, R. 2000. Female athletes face unique injury risk. *USA Today*, Nov. 1, 2000.

elements, combined with the more traditional workout regimens, will give athletes an even better result from their training.

The Jumpmetrics plan is dedicated to providing an athlete with state-of-the-art exercise design. The plan was developed based on knowledge provided by a group of physical therapists, athletic trainers, and strength and conditioning specialists. These experts in the field realized that due to stresses placed on the body by the extremes of athletic activity, athletes' muscles are often out of correct balance. This lack of muscle balance can cause tightness in some muscles, making the muscles that assist them overly loose or weak. These imbalances often lead to joint misalignment and momentary loss of body control. This loss of control can eventually lead to injury. At the base of the Jumpmetrics plan is a critically important evaluation system that is used to determine an athlete's physical limitations and to determine how the athlete should proceed through the levels of the training program. The goal of the evaluation is to fully identify the "weak links" an athlete has throughout his or her body so the athlete can attempt to improve those weaknesses before they lead to injury. Jumpmetrics provides exercises designed specifically to target the weak areas and to fine-tune the athlete into being a safe performer. The plan provides a system that empowers the athlete against time-consuming or career-ending injuries and also provides several training packages to assist athletes in reaching their body's maximal speed, agility, and power potential.

Sports programs often become overfocused on the big picture of winning, and strength and conditioning coaches are forced to design programs with unbalanced objectives. If you are an excellent athlete, you may think that you don't have a high potential for injury, but remember that even Michael Jordan had to have surgery near the end of his career. Constantly striving to improve yourself physically by maintaining appropriate muscular balance will allow you to have a longer career. If you are a young and developing athlete who continually suffers with aches, pains, or general fatigue, and you are often missing workouts due to nagging injuries, then you are like 90 percent of your fellow athletes, and you need the solution the Jumpmetrics system provides.

What to Expect From Jumpmetrics

During this jump and power enhancement program, you will perform exercises and drills that are intended to improve performance in each of these categories: general movement/warm-up, balance, power, strength, and flexibility. You will be instructed on position, form, and posture in each exercise and drill. From this you will gain a higher understanding of what your body is supposed to be doing and what you should feel during any sports-related movement.

You will not experience conditioning. You will not experience extreme (only some) cardiorespiratory or muscular fatigue-based conditioning. You will not complete the workout feeling totally exhausted; after all, this plan is often implemented as a pre- and postpractice routine. Our intention with this program is to make you more aware of what your body is supposed to feel like when the movement is performed correctly. We are seeking the quality in each movement, rather than quantity purely for the purpose of exhausting you. Perfect practice makes for movement perfection. Fatigued practice makes for erratic and imperfect movement. Your strength and conditioning coach and sport coaches should provide you with all the conditioning you will need in conjunction with this specialization program.

Before beginning this or any other written program, you must realize that it will never be as good as receiving one-on-one instruction from a qualified coach. In a book, photos can show the exercises, but the skills required to optimize that exercise must be continuously refined. Constant cueing from a coach with a trained eye will ensure that you are in the correct posture, and the smaller things that usually go wrong and waste precious time are minimized. Sometimes locating or affording good coaching is difficult. This is why we have designed this written program to be as comprehensive as possible. In *Jumpmetrics,* we have tried to provide complete and digestible training knowledge that will cover all the physical components of becoming the ultimate athlete.

Assessing Your Athletic Alignment and Performance Posture

Posture is body position either characteristic or assumed for a special purpose. In this book, we differentiate between posture that is *characteristic* and posture that is *assumed* for a special purpose. Characteristic posture is what you commonly think of when you hear the word *posture*. Do you have flat feet? Is your head forward or do you tend to slouch when you stand? Your parents were right when they said posture is very important in how we all function. If you have bad posture, you will be less effective as an athlete. Assumed posture refers to getting into and out of different positions based on your sport. Do you have good posture when you jump, cut, sprint, and so on? If you don't, or you're not sure, then chances are you are not maximizing your potential as an athlete, and worse, you may be placing yourself in potentially harmful situations.

Optimal posture and alignment help to provide good shock absorption, assist in weight acceptance, and promote the transfer of energy during movement (figure 1.1). In other words, optimal posture allows the body to move more efficiently, fatigue less easily, and place less stress on the joints. Optimal posture will assist in the prevention of overtraining, muscle imbalances, and decreased performance.

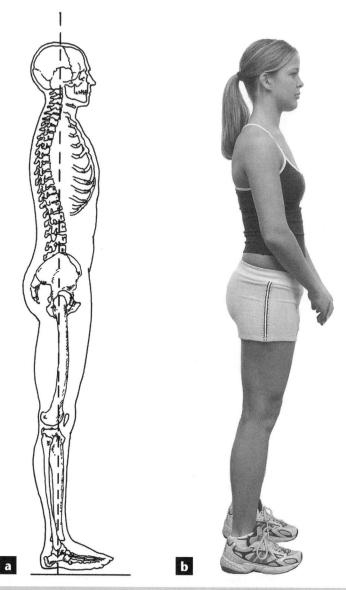

Figure 1.1 *(a)* Optimal posture, side view: A line should fall from the middle of the ear, through the center of the shoulder, middle of the femur, and just behind the knee and lateral malleolus; *(b)* Athlete demonstrating optimal posture for best muscle balance.

Posture helps determine which muscles are strong and weak by lengthening or shortening certain muscles. There is an optimum length at which the muscle is capable of developing maximal tension (figure 1.2). Muscles are made up of small fibers called *actin* and *myosin*. When you want a muscle to contract, these fibers connect and pull the muscle fibers closer together. To generate the strongest contractions, actin and myosin fibers must be positioned at an ideal length. If a muscle is too short, the actin and myosin fibers can meet but do not have room to contract or shorten. If the muscles are too long or excessively lengthened, the actin and myosin fibers cannot make enough contact to cause a significant contraction.

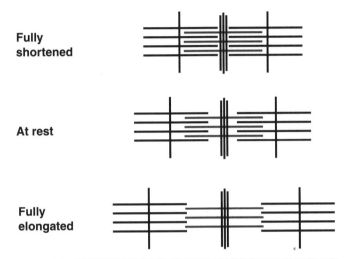

Fully shortened

At rest

Fully elongated

Figure 1.2 Diagram illustrating optimal muscle length. Top (shortened muscle)—actin and myosin muscle fibers are too close to effectively contract, thus making the muscle functionally weaker. Middle (muscle with good balance)—actin and myosin muscle fibers are at the correct length apart to connect and shorten to create a good muscular contraction. Lower (lengthened muscle)—actin and myosin fibers are too far apart to effectively contract once they attach, thus making the muscle functionally weaker.

Let's define some common characteristic posture types so you can see which one closely resembles yours. If you have one of these characteristic postures or have some components of one, you will have some typical areas that need to be stronger. The workouts described throughout this book help alleviate any weak links.

Posture 1: Hyperlordosis

Hyperlordosis is defined as an excessive anterior tilting of the pelvis (figure 1.3). This places increased stress on the low back region. One of the most common causes of this excessive tilting is weak muscles around the lower abdominal region. Other characteristics of this posture are sagging shoulders, thighs rotated slightly inward, and a slight protrusion of the head. This is all done to maintain the body's center of gravity. With hyperlordotic posture, the athlete will often have tight hip flexors, tight side hip muscles (tensor fascia latae), and weak lower abdominals. Remember that tight hip flexors (muscles on the front of your hip) will shorten your stride when running and cause you to run slower.

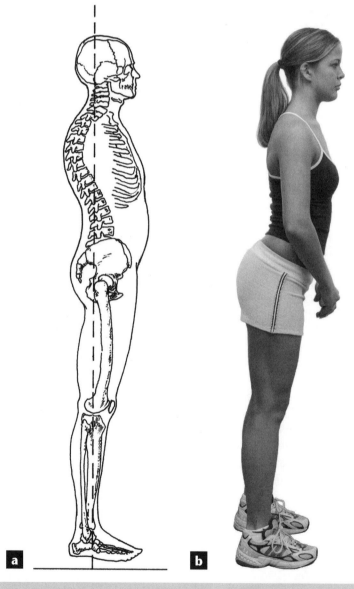

a   b

Figure 1.3 (*a*) Diagram of hyperlordotic posture. (*b*) Athlete demonstrating hyperlordosis. Athletes with this posture will have tight hip flexors, tight side hip muscles (tensor fascia latae), and weak lower abdominals.

Posture 2: Swayback Deformity

Swayback deformity is a postural malformation that involves excessive arching of the lower (lumbar) spine, with the upper back (thoracic spine) exhibiting a roundness or kyphosis (figure 1.4). With the deformity, the hips shoot forward, causing the hips to move into extension. Again, to maintain the body's center of gravity, the upper back rounds. An athlete with a swayback posture will often have tight hip extensors (hip rotators and hamstrings) and tight low back muscles. The athlete will often have weak hip flexors, weak lower abdominals, and weak shoulder blade muscles. These athletes are less likely to be powerful and explosive due to this posture type.

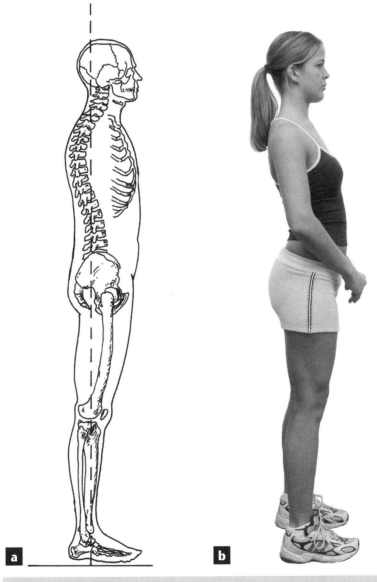

Figure 1.4 *(a)* Diagram of swayback posture. *(b)* Athlete demonstrating swayback posture. Athletes with this posture will have tight hip extensors (hip rotators and hamstrings) and tight low back muscles. Weak hip flexors, lower abdominals, and shoulder blade muscles are also common.

Posture 3: Flat Back

Flat back posture is a malformation in which the athlete has a decreased curve in the low back region (figure 1.5). An athlete with this posture will have tight hip muscles and weak low back and hip flexor muscles.

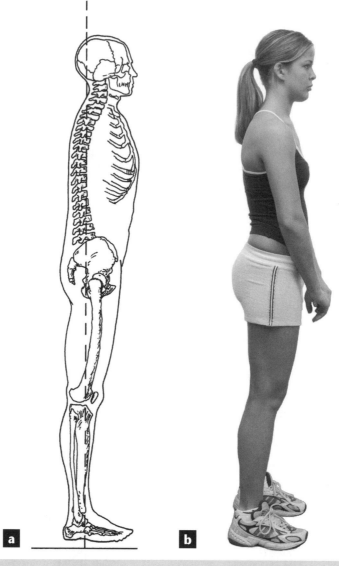

Figure 1.5 *(a)* Diagram of flat back posture. *(b)* Athlete demonstrating flat back posture. Athletes with this posture often have tight side hip muscles, weak lower back muscles, and weak hip flexors.

Posture 4: Pronated Posture

A pronated posture is determined by looking from the front and checking the position of the athlete's arches and knee alignment in relation to the feet. Athletes with a pronated posture will have flat arches and their knees and thighbones (femurs) will be positioned inward (varus position). Any of these deviations from proper alignment will put more stress on the knee and signal that this athlete needs some extra strength and conditioning. This posture also makes it more difficult to move quickly.

Athletes who display a varus or "knee-in" posture on landings and takeoffs when running or jumping may be more susceptible to knee injuries. Some may argue this point, stating that the inward movement at the knee places a more pronounced stretch on the external rotators of the hip (resulting in a greater influence of the stretch-shortening cycle in the muscle group, thus leading to greater jumping ability). It is true that an inward tracking of the knee can contribute to greater reflex potential, and if the athlete is knowledgeable of the position of the knee and is able to control this motion, it may be acceptable in some athletic situations to let the knee move inward. However, this knee position is not recommended for two reasons. First, when the knees track inward, smaller muscles (those found in the external rotator group) are used to produce reflexive power. With proper knee position, much larger muscles (the quadriceps group) are used to create and absorb more force. Second, if the knees are positioned inside the big toe, the ground force is not distributed effectively throughout the lower body (instead, the force moves directly into the middle portion of the knee). The middle portion of the knee is required to manage the jumping and landing forces alone, and the knees may be injured or overworked as a result. Keeping the knees in line with the second or third toe of the foot can help to better distribute the forces being generated. With this knee position, force is initiated through the lower leg, and this helps to effectively activate the muscles of the lower legs and the quadriceps of the upper leg (resulting in potentially greater jumping ability).

Another component of posture can be checked by observing an athlete from the side and noticing whether the knees bend backward or hyperextend. If an athlete's knees bend backward in his standing posture, it means that his hamstring muscles are on a constant stretch and may not react quickly to help protect the knees during jumping, cutting, and defensive drills. This may also be an indication that his hamstrings are weak and need extra focus during the strengthening (overload) portions of the workout plans described in this book. During the evaluation process, any deviations in knee alignment should be noted in the single-leg stance section of the evaluation chart (table 2.1 on page 24).

How do these postures affect your performance? If you have any of these postures or some components of a couple of different postures, don't worry too much. Your job is to become aware of these postures and keep them from causing your muscles to become tight or weak. These postures will not affect your performance unless you have trouble getting into your sports postures. Try to "assume" these postures so you can feel the exaggerated positions and see which posture most closely resembles your own. Remember, muscles have to be at their ideal length to be the most powerful. This means that if a muscle is too tight or too long (excessive flexibility) it cannot contract effectively, and the net result is loss of power, or worse—an injury. Tight or weak muscles also make an athlete less effective by causing poor movement patterns.

Defensive Position

Let's look at how an athlete gets into a defensive or athletic stance. This should involve hinging at the hips to "sit back." Figure 1.6 shows an athlete in an improper defensive stance (bent at the waist). This position will cause

Figure 1.6 Athlete demonstrating a defensive stance with rounded upper back. This poor position will not allow the athlete to use her hips effectively to move from side to side.

Figure 1.7 Good defensive position with back in straight line and athlete appropriately bent at the hips to engage the muscles of her lower extremity more effectively.

her to lose lateral quickness because she cannot engage her hip muscles effectively. In addition, she will lose stability at her knees because this upright posture makes her hips functionally weaker. Figure 1.7 shows an athlete in a good "hip-hinged" position. Notice the straightness of the spine and how the athlete is bent more at the hips so she can engage them for increased quickness, agility, and acceleration.

One method that can be used to assess and teach proper defensive position is to take a stick (e.g., a dowel rod, golf club, or broom stick) and place it on the athlete's back. Position the stick so that it touches the buttocks and the back of the head (figure 1.8).

The athlete then squats, holding on to the stick with the top hand. If the athlete hinges properly at the hips, the stick stays on his back (figure 1.9). If the athlete bends at the waist, the stick will come away from the back (figure 1.10). This indicates poor posture when trying to assume the athletic or defensive position.

Figure 1.8 Start position for teaching the "hip hinge" or how to achieve a good defensive position. Notice that the stick is in contact with the head and buttocks.

Figure 1.9 Correct squat into a good defensive position. Notice that the stick never left the lower back.

Figure 1.10 Incorrect method to achieve a good defensive position. Notice how the athlete rounds his upper back, causing the stick to come away from the buttocks region. Ultimately, this will place the athlete in a poor position, and he will not be able to use the muscles of his hips and lower extremity in an effective manner.

The second item to check when assessing proper athletic or defensive posture is the position of the knees. To assess this, the athlete should squat into the defensive stance, keeping the back straight up and down, and allowing the knees to extend over the toes. When the athlete is squatting, look at the position of the knees (figure 1.11). From the front, observe the direction of the knees when ascending or descending from the squat.

Figure 1.11 *(a)* Knees in good position while achieving a defensive stance (knees should always track over the second and third toes). *(b)* Knees in poor position while achieving a defensive stance (knees are tracking inside the first toes, placing more stress on the knee joints).

The knees should track over the second and third toes while squatting. The knees may track inward for many reasons, but two common reasons are lack of awareness of the technique and lack of strength in the hips. Inward tracking of the kneecaps places a great deal of stress on the knee and is a major contributor to decreased jumping potential and an increase in knee injuries. Inward tracking is also a sign that the athlete may have hip weakness and may be unable to control rotational forces in the knee.

A third area to assess athletic posture is in the backpedaling motion. As the athlete backpedals, observe the position of the spine (figure 1.12). Is it rounded or straight? Failure to have good posture during this drill will decrease an athlete's reaction time to turn and run.

Figure 1.12 *(a)* Good backpedaling posture (notice how the back is straight and hinged at the hips). *(b)* Bad backpedaling posture (notice how the back is rounded).

The postures discussed earlier (hyperlordotic, swayback, flat back, and pronated) are important for three reasons. First, these postures cause certain muscle imbalances in the spine and hips that make the athlete weaker. Second, these postures make it more difficult for athletes to achieve an ideal posture in their defensive position. For example, an athlete with a flat back posture will have excessive roundness in the back when he is in the defensive position (figure 1.13). An athlete with hyperlordotic posture will exhibit excessive arching of the lower (lumbar) spine during the athletic or defensive position. This will often cause early fatigue and cause the athlete to stay up taller. When staying up taller, the athlete will not be as effective with cutting or change of direction movements.

The third reason an athlete must be aware of these postures is that if the pelvis is not in a good position, the muscles are not at their ideal length and are thus functionally weaker. Because the hips control stress on the knees, if the hips are weak, then additional stress is placed on the knee.

Figure 1.13 Athletes with flat back posture will often have a rounded back when they try to achieve a defensive position.

The type of posture you have determines which muscles in your body will be tight or weak. Muscles function best when they operate at their optimal length. For example, an athlete with excessive lordosis will often have weak lower abdominals and tight hip flexors (front hip muscles). These deficiencies will make the athlete less likely to get into the athletic postures necessary to optimize her performance.

As an athlete, you should always be aware of how you "carry yourself" (i.e., your posture). This knowledge, combined with the knowledge of how to achieve a good defensive position, squat, and backpedal, will instantaneously make you move better.

Take the Jumpmetrics screening tests in chapter 2 to see whether you are functioning at or near your potential.

2

Evaluating Your Jumping and Athletic Potential and Functional Flexibility

Have you ever seen Vince Carter fly through the air to dunk a basketball? His vertical jump is 42 inches. Have you seen Mia Hamm jump up at the perfect time to head a ball into the goal? Both athletes are very strong but also know how to use their bodies to achieve optimal performance. Following the easy-to-administer tests in this chapter will allow you to discover your "weak links." You will be able to score yourself and follow a detailed plan to overcome any deficits. If you are a coach, you've seen your athletes perform drills, run sprints, jump, and cut. You know which athletes move gracefully and which do not. You know which athletes are stronger and which

The scoring system for the following tests is on a scale of 1 to 3. However, three of the tests are considered to be higher predictors of poor performance and injury potential—single-leg squat, landing technique, and single-leg hop. The scores for these tests are doubled to signify their importance.

tire more easily. This knowledge—and the tests and visual skills taught in this chapter—will allow you to screen your athletes and help them train at a higher level.

Another aspect of athletic potential is flexibility. A second set of tests in this chapter will help you to see where improvements can be made in flexibility. Along with the tests are corrective stretches that should help you achieve optimum flexibility.

Test 1: Single-Leg Stance (Alignment)

The first item to be assessed is the arch of the foot (figure 2.1). The athlete should lift one leg so that the thigh is parallel with the ground (figure 2.2) and try to balance in this position for 30 seconds. While the athlete is in this position, examine the lower foot. Notice if the arch of the foot flattens or stays relatively unchanged. Excessive flattening of the arch is an indication that the athlete cannot control his own body weight, and this will be amplified with running, jumping, and cutting. There should be ample space (approximately a half inch) between the arch of the foot and the floor. If the feet are flat (figure 2.3), then there is some extra stress on the shin (tibia) and knee.

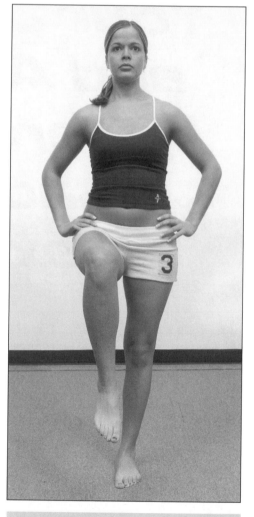

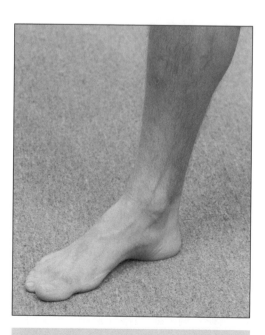

Figure 2.1 Assessment of foot posture. Notice whether the arch is flat, appropriate, or excessive. This arch is considered to be of appropriate height and would be scored a 3 if held during the single-leg stance.

Figure 2.2 Single-leg stance with thigh parallel to the ground to assess balance and what happens to the arch while balancing.

Any athlete with "flat feet" should be advised on proper footwear, which includes shoes that help to decrease pronation. Most shoe manufacturers have shoes that are designed for this function. Athletes who have extremely flat feet may benefit from custom shoe inserts or orthotics. (Seek medical advice if you think you may benefit from a custom shoe insert.) Likewise, if the athlete has excessive arches ("high arch"), she too should be advised on proper footwear. The shoe for an athlete with a high arch is one that has slightly more cushion to help dampen some of the forces that are imparted on the foot during running and jumping.

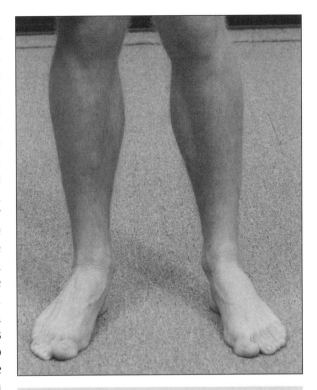

Figure 2.3 Athlete with flat arches who would be a candidate for orthotic intervention. This athlete would be scored a 1.

Scores

The athlete receives a score of 1 for a flat arch or one that looks normal but collapses when the single-leg stance is achieved. A score of 2 is given for a high arch or if the foot rolls toward the outside continuously during the single-leg stance test. A score of 3 is achieved when the arch is maintained and good balance is noted.

Test 2: Single-Leg Squat (Double Scoring)

A second area to address is lower extremity alignment when the athlete performs a single-leg squat. Figure 2.4 shows an athlete performing a single-leg squat with proper form. Notice the position of the knee in relation to the middle toe. Ideally, the knee should track in alignment with the middle toe. Inward tracking of the knee is a sign that the athlete has some weakness or lack of control of the hip muscles (figure 2.5). This "falling in" of the knee places major stress on the knee and the anterior cruciate ligament (ACL). The lack of control during a single-leg squat is an indication that the athlete may not be ready to participate in drills or activities that require repetitive jumping. Any repetitive jumps or drills that occur when the athlete becomes fatigued will cause additional stress to the knee because these require more control than a static single-leg squat. Finally, inward tracking of the knee will decrease vertical jump height because the forces at the knees are acting more medially (toward the middle) than vertically.

Scores

The athlete receives a score of 1 if the knee tracks over the inside of the foot (figure 2.5). A score of 4 is given if the kneecap moves inward over the first toe (figure 2.6). A score of 6 is given if the kneecap tracks squarely over the second and third toes (figure 2.4).

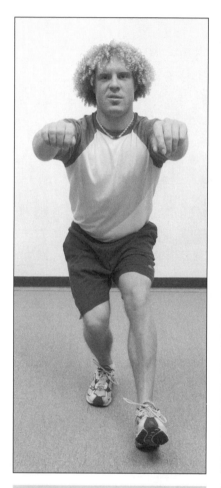

Figure 2.4 Athlete demonstrating good single-leg squat with the kneecap tracking in alignment with the second and third toes. This athlete would receive a score of 6.

Figure 2.5 Poor single-leg squat with the knee tracking on the inside of the first toe. This athlete would receive a score of 1.

Figure 2.6 Single-leg squat with knee tracking over the first toe. This athlete would receive a score of 4.

Test 3: Jumping and Test 4: Landing (Double Scoring for Test 4)

This part of the screening is used to evaluate how the athlete jumps and lands using both feet. When the athlete squats to jump, the knees should track over the second and third toes (figure 2.7). The athlete should land with the knees tracking over the middle toes and with the knees bent between 30 and 40 degrees. Landing with significantly less flexion or knee bend negates the action of the hamstring muscles (back of thigh).

Let's discuss briefly the action of the hamstring muscles. When an athlete jumps and lands, the major muscle used is the quadriceps (front of thigh). Because of their attachment to the shinbone, the quadriceps causes the tibia to be pulled in a forward direction. The hamstrings have to supply an equivalent backward force to prevent excessive stress from being placed on the anterior cruciate ligament (ACL) of the knee. The hamstrings originate from the lower part of the pelvis and run down the back of the leg to insert into the back of the tibia (shinbone). When the muscle contracts, it stabilizes the tibia and does not let the tibia slide forward. If the knee is straight upon landing, this stabilization is lost because the angle of pull causes more compression and less backward pull.

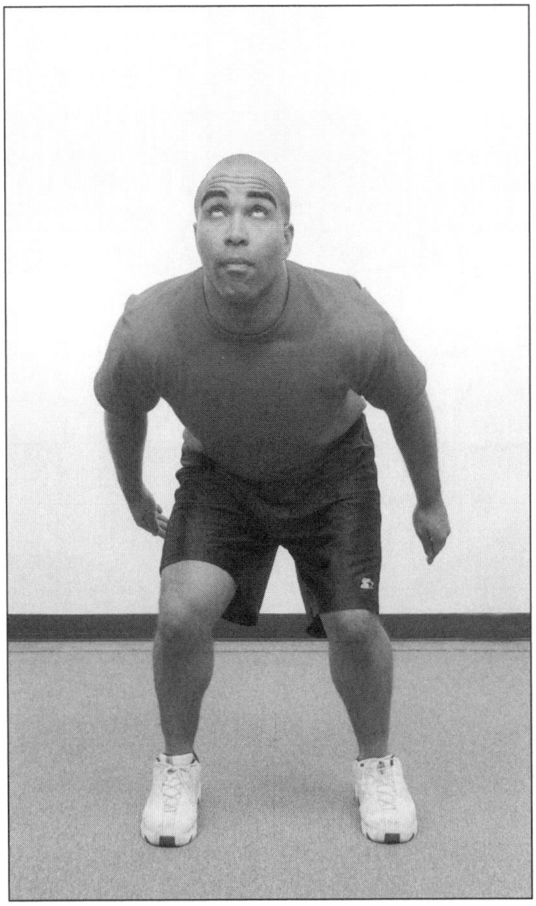

To perform test 3 and 4 together, the athlete should jump up as high as he can and repeat 10 times without a break between jumps. Observe how the athlete starts his jump (knee position) and how he lands. Any repetition in which the athlete's knee or knees track medially or inward indicates lack of control of the knee, and the athlete may be at risk for tearing the anterior cruciate ligament.

Figure 2.7 Athlete squatting to jump. This athlete would receive a score of 3 (on test 3) since his knees track over his second and third toes. If the athlete landed from the jump with his knees in this position, he would receive a score of 6 on test 4.

Scores

For either test, the athlete is given a score of 1 if the knee tracks inside the first toe (figure 2.8). For test 3, a score of 2 is given if the knee tracks over the first toe upon jumping (figure 2.9), and a score of 3 is given when the knees track over the second and third toes (figure 2.7). Proper landing is such a critical aspect of absorbing shock and preparing the athlete to jump again that scores are doubled for test 4—a score of 4 is given if the knee tracks over the first toe, and a score of 6 if the knee tracks over the second and third toes (figure 2.10).

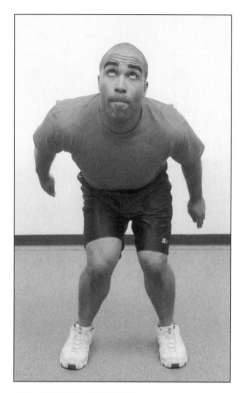

Figure 2.8 An athlete jumping or landing with the knees tracking inside the first toe receives a score of 1.

Figure 2.9 Athlete jumping with the knees tracking over the first toe. A score of 2 is given on test 3 for this posture. If the athlete lands with the knees tracking over the first toe, a score of 4 is given on test 4.

Figure 2.10 Athlete landing with the knees tracking over the second and third toes. A score of 6 is given on test 4 for this posture.

Test 5: Single-Leg Hop (Double Scoring)

A fifth area to examine is single-leg hopping by the athlete. The athlete should hop forward on one leg and "freeze" upon landing. Observe the position of the knee upon landing. Did the knee land in a bent position? Did the kneecap track over the second toe or come inward? This test is slightly more advanced than the single-leg squat and gives a good indication of whether the athlete can control her knee in a more dynamic situation.

Scores

The athlete is given a score of 1 if the knee tracks inside the first toe upon landing (figure 2.11). A score of 4 is given if the knee tracks over the first toe either upon landing or jumping (figure 2.12). Finally, a score of 6 is given if the athlete can jump and land on one leg with the knee tracking over the second and third toes (figure 2.13).

Figure 2.11 Athlete finishing his single-leg hop with his knee tracking inside the first toe. A score of 1 is given for this hop.

Figure 2.12 Athlete finishing his single-leg hop with his knee tracking over the first toe. A score of 4 is given for this hop.

Figure 2.13 Athlete finishing his single-leg hop with his knee tracking in alignment with the second and third toes. A score of 6 is given for this hop.

Test 6: Hamstring Curls

The sixth area to examine is the strength of the hamstring muscles. On a flat leg curl machine, the athlete should be able to perform a single-leg leg curl with 40 percent of her body weight (figure 2.14). Failure to perform a one-legged leg curl with 40 percent of the athlete's body weight will confirm a strength deficit, and additional work will need to be done for this region.

Scores

A score of 1 is given if the athlete cannot perform a single-leg leg curl with 40 percent of her body weight. A score of 2 is given if the athlete can curl 40 percent of her body weight, and a score of 3 is given if the athlete can achieve a single-leg leg curl with greater than 40 percent of her body weight.

Figure 2.14 One-leg curl. A score of 1 is given if the athlete cannot curl 40 percent of her body weight, a 2 for curling 40 percent of her body weight, and a 3 for curling greater than 40 percent of her body weight.

Test 7: Pelvis Lift (Bridge)

The final area to be examined is the strength of the lower trunk muscles (abdominals and lower back) that control rotational forces in the body. The trunk muscles play a key role in keeping the lower quarter stable. When the knee becomes injured, it is often because of the athlete's inability to control the rotational forces in the lower extremity. Research shows that the transverse abdominis is the first muscle to fire when performing any type of resistive activity. To test for rotational control, the athlete will get into a "bridge" position (figure 2.15). This position is achieved by lifting the pelvis off the floor so that a straight line runs from the knees to the chest. Make sure the athlete's lumbar spine or low back is not extended or arched (figure 2.16).

Figure 2.15   Good bridge position. Hips are level and a straight line can be drawn from the knees to the shoulders.

Figure 2.16   Excessive arching when trying to achieve a bridge position.

While maintaining this position, the athlete should keep the pelvis level and try not to let the pelvis drop or tilt to one side. Hands are held across the chest, and the athlete lifts one knee approximately one inch off the floor (just high enough to get the foot off the floor; see figure 2.17). Observe whether the athlete can keep the pelvis level when the knee is raised.

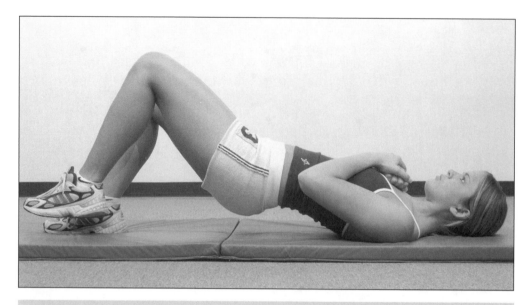

Figure 2.17 Athlete demonstrates good trunk rotational strength by lifting one foot and keeping the pelvis level. If the athlete feels this work her back, a score of 2 would be given. If the athlete does not feel this exercise work the low back muscles, then she would receive a score of 3.

Scores

If the athlete cannot keep the pelvis level when one knee is raised, the athlete is given a score of 1 (figure 2.18). If the athlete can lift one knee and keep the pelvis level but feels the exercise work the low back muscles, this is given a score of 2 (this is also an indication that the lower abdominals are not firing appropriately and the athlete is compensating to perform the movement). Maintaining a level pelvis is scored as a 3 if the athlete reports that he does not feel the exercise work the lower back muscles.

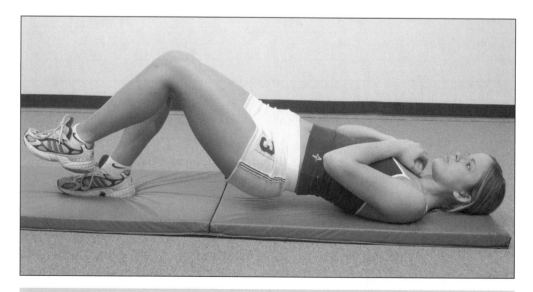

Figure 2.18 Athlete demonstrating poor trunk rotational strength. When she lifted her right foot, her pelvis fell toward that side. This would receive a score of 1.

Understanding Your Scores

The score for the seven areas should be recorded and totaled in table 2.1. Based on the range that the total score falls within, the athlete is determined to be at low risk, potential risk, or at risk for a noncontact knee injury. A poor score on a single category does not, by itself, predispose an athlete to injury. A low total score on the evaluation as a whole, however, does indicate a higher level of weakness and a lower level of neuromuscular control that could result in increased stress on the knees, hips, and ankles. These stressors are warning flags to the athlete that injury potential and decreased physical performance are present. In the following chapters, exercises that address all these areas will be described, and after several weeks of training, the screening can be completed again to check improvement.

Key:
    25-30 = low risk athlete
    11-24 = potential risk athlete
     7-10 = at-risk athlete

An athlete's total score on the evaluation will determine how the athlete proceeds through the levels in the Jumpmetrics workout plans. For the individual athlete using the workouts on his own, the workout plans should be completed as follows:

 • **If the athlete scores in the *at-risk* scoring range,** the athlete must begin at level 1 and then progress through each level until completion. After level 1 has been completed, the evaluation should be administered again; if the athlete scores poorly on the first five exercises on the evaluation, he must repeat level 1.

 • **If the athlete scores in the *potential risk* scoring range,** the athlete must go through the level 1 training for two weeks before advancing to complete the level 2 and 3 workout plans.

 • **If the athlete scores in the *low risk* scoring range,** the athlete must go through the level 1 training for one week and through level 2 training for two weeks before advancing to complete the level 3 workout plan.

In a team environment where a coach is trying to supervise many athletes at once, the athletes should complete the entire Jumpmetrics plan from levels 1 to 3 in its entirety.

Focusing on Functional Flexibility

Flexibility is the ability to adapt, and it is another key to reaching your potential as an athlete. This "adaptiveness" is significant because the muscles must be able to lengthen and shorten on a moment's notice. The inability to make this change is the reason muscles are pulled and joints become injured. Ideal flexibility means having enough range of motion in the muscles and joints to promote performance while having enough flexibility to decrease the chance of injury. The rest of this chapter includes tests for each area of the body and explains what it means to have good flexibility and why

TABLE 2.1

Screening the Athlete

Test	Alignment			Left	Right
Single-leg stance (Hold for 30 seconds) (Scale of 1 to 3)	Feet flat **1**	High arch **2**	Normal **3**		
Single-leg squat** (Scale of 1 to 6)	Knee tracks over inside foot. **1**	Knee tracks over first toe. **4**	Knee tracks over second and third toes. **6**		
Jumping technique (Perform 10 reps) (Scale of 1 to 3)	Knees travel inward. **1**	Knees track over first toe. **2**	Knees track over second and third toes. **3**		
Landing technique** (Perform 10 reps) (Scale of 1 to 6)	Knees bend but only slightly. **1**	Knees bend >30 degrees but track inward. **4**	Knees bend >30 degrees and track over second and third toes. **6**		
Single-leg hop** (Scale of 1 to 6)	Knee tracks inside first toe. **1**	Knee tracks over first toe. **4**	Knee tracks over second and third toes. **6**		
Hamstring curls (Scale of 1 to 3)	Less than 40% body weight. **1**	Equal to 40% body weight. **2**	Greater than 40% body weight. **3**		
Pelvis lift (Bridge) (Scale of 1 to 3)	Cannot lift one knee and keep pelvis level. **1**	Can lift one knee and keep pelvis level but low back muscles work. **2**	Can lift one knee and keep pelvis level with no stress on the back. **3**		
SCORING 25-30 = Low risk athlete 11-24 = Potential risk athlete 7-10 = At-risk athlete			**Total**		

** Signifies increase importance in assessment. Middle and high scores are doubled.

sometimes too much flexibility (especially in the hamstrings and hips) can make muscles less reactive and decrease your performance.

The most common flexibility enhancement programs use static stretching to improve muscle length. Jumpmetrics employs static stretching techniques as a means of correcting the inflexible problem areas revealed to you on the Jumpmetrics evaluation. Static stretching reduces excessive movement during the stretching exercise, and the final depths of the stretch are held at full muscle length for an assigned amount of time. Static stretching is essential to creating a permanent increase in muscle length. However, static stretching is sometimes misplaced in the athlete's training program. Although static stretching is a very effective method of improving flexibility, it should be used sparingly at the beginning of a workout session. Static flexibility training can leave the muscle feeling very loose and unresponsive. Muscles that have lost some of their tension ratios and feel less secure can lead to momentary losses of muscle control and can lead to injury.

To understand how proper flexibility can help your performance, consider the following analogy:

Two cars are racing on a speedway at 100 miles per hour. From the outside, they both look equally fast. However, if you take a look at each car's tachometer, you discover something surprising. Both cars are traveling at the same speed, but one car's engine is running at 3,000 RPM, while the other car's engine is running at 8,000 RPM. Which car is working harder to achieve its level of performance? Which car is more likely to break down? Obviously, the car running at 8,000 RPM is not as efficient as the car at 3,000 RPM. In a similar manner, poor flexibility makes your body work harder to achieve the same performance. Over time this lack of flexibility will cause your body to fail you. Perform the following tests to see which areas you need to improve. These tests involve areas where athletes often have some limitations—areas that are commonly weak links in an athlete's overall physical performance.

Note: You will need a parent, coach, or teammate to assist you with some of these tests.

Area 1: Big Toe

The first area to be examined for flexibility is the big toe. Stiffness of this area will cause your foot to roll in and subsequently place more stress on your knee when you jump and run. A typical sign of this stiffness is a callus on the inside of the toe. When an athlete runs, the foot needs to hinge at the big toe joint. Failure to have adequate flexibility at this joint will cause the foot to roll in during the push-off phase of walking or running. Over time a callus will develop due to the increased friction occurring on the inside of the big toe. This doesn't seem like a significant problem, but this inward rotation of the foot (flattening of the arch) also causes the knee to rotate inward. If the knee tracks inward rather than over the second toe, running and jumping capabilities are diminished. Limitation of the big toe is also one of the leading causes of turf toe (an irritation of the joint in the big toe commonly seen in athletes who play on hard surfaces such as artificial turf).

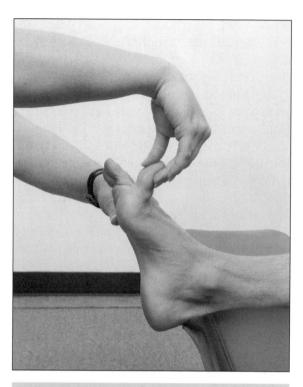

Figure 2.19 Big toe flexibility assessment. Tightness will affect the way you run and cut.

Test

To test big toe flexibility, a partner should push your foot up to form a right angle with your lower leg. While maintaining this right angle, the partner will push your big toe toward your knee (figure 2.19). The big toe should go back 45 degrees. Any difficulty in achieving this position should be noted, and the following corrective stretch should be initiated.

Corrective Stretch for Stiffness of the Big Toe

Sit on the floor with one leg pulled in with the knee bent. Pull the foot up to form a right angle with the lower leg. Place one hand on the big toe and pull outward slightly to create some distraction at the joint. Pull the toe up toward the kneecap while maintaining this distraction (figure 2.20). You should feel a slight stretch but no pain. Hold this stretch for 30 seconds and repeat three times on either side that is found to be restricted.

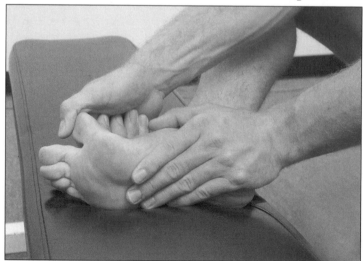

Figure 2.20 Corrective stretch for big toe stiffness. Make sure to distract the toe slightly before you bend the toe upward.

Area 2: Ankle Joint

Inflexibility at the ankle joint will also cause the foot to roll inward excessively (pronate) and lead to decreased performance with running and jumping. Tightness can also lead to shinsplints and Achilles tendinitis.

Test

Keep your leg and knee straight and muscles relaxed. A partner grasps the top of your foot and pulls back toward your knee. With your knee straight, your foot should easily go past a right angle (figure 2.21). Tightness means you will need to perform some calf stretching to address this deficit. While in the same position, bend your knee slightly and have your partner stabilize the knee by placing his fist under the raised knee; your foot should now move more toward your knee (figure 2.22). If your foot doesn't travel one to two inches past the 90-degree mark, this indicates that your soleus muscle (the muscle underneath your calf muscle) is tight.

Tightness in these areas means that when performing a squat, it will be difficult to keep the heels down or the feet will roll in causing the knees to also shift inward (figure 2.23).

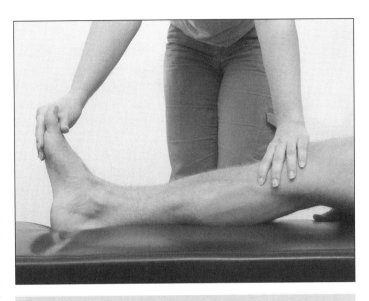

Figure 2.21 Calf (gastrocnemius) assessment. The knee is held in a straight position and the foot should go past 90 degrees or a right angle. This athlete demonstrates some tightness of the calf muscle group.

Figure 2.23 Athletes with tight calves will often let their feet roll in when squatting. Any athlete that squats like this should be examined for tightness in the ankle joints and calves.

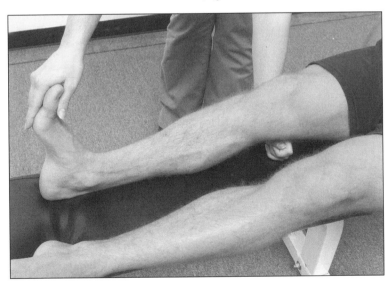

Figure 2.22 Calf (soleus) assessment. The knee is bent by a teammate or coach placing a fist under the knee. Your foot should bend more toward your knee when the knee is bent.

Corrective Stretches for Stiff Ankle Joints and Tight Calves

Stand facing a wall and step back with one leg. Place both hands on the wall to brace yourself. While standing, put one leg in front of the other and lean forward to rest your hands against the wall. Make sure your back leg is straight and the back foot is turned inward (figure 2.24). Allow your body to come forward toward the wall, keeping your feet in their original positions. You should feel a stretch in the back of your calf. After holding this stretch for 30 seconds, allow your back knee to bend (figure 2.25). This will shift the stretch to the Achilles. Hold this stretch for 30 seconds, then repeat both stretches with the other leg. To increase the intensity of the stretch, turn your body to the left or right while holding the stretch. This rotational component is the most effective method for adding intensity to any stretch.

Figure 2.24 Calf stretch with the knee straight and the back foot turned slightly inward.

Figure 2.25 Calf stretch with the back knee bent and the back foot turned slightly inward. You should feel this stretch more around your Achilles region.

Area 3: Quadriceps

Inflexibility in the quadriceps area places excessive stress on the kneecap and can lead to pain in the front of the knee. Effective jumpers should expect to have some quadriceps tightness because of the repetitive jumping that many athletes perform. Only when this tightness is excessive will it present a problem.

Test

To check for tightness, lie on your belly and bend your knee to bring your foot toward your buttocks. As your foot gets closer, reach back and grab the foot with your same side hand. Pull your foot all the way up to touch your buttocks (figure 2.26). You should have some slight difficulty pulling your foot to your buttocks, but it should be able to touch. If it is very easy for you to touch and you don't feel much stretch in the front of your thigh, you may be overly flexible in your quads, and you will need to emphasize quadriceps strengthening in the overload section of the Jumpmetrics workout plan. If you have difficulty, try the following stretch.

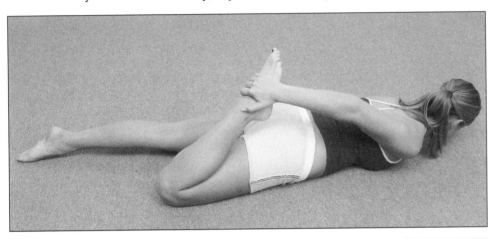

Figure 2.26 Quadriceps assessment. You should be able to pull your heel to your buttocks but have some resistance.

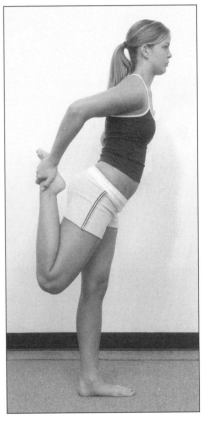

Corrective Stretch for Quadriceps Tightness

In a standing position, bend one knee so that your foot comes toward your buttocks. Reach behind your body with one hand and grab the foot to bring it as close as possible to your buttocks (figure 2.27). To increase the intensity of this stretch, pull your knee farther behind you. Stop once you feel the stretch increase, and hold for 30 seconds. Repeat for two repetitions.

Figure 2.27 Corrective stretch for quadriceps tightness. Make sure your knee is pointing behind you to increase the stretch.

Area 4: Hamstrings

The hamstrings (muscles on the back of the legs) assist in controlling the forces at the knee when running and jumping. The hamstrings are often tight in males, but in the female athlete they have a tendency to be overly flexible.

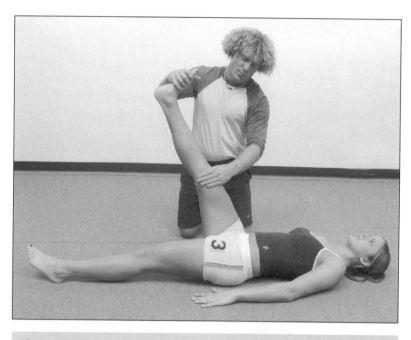

Figure 2.28 Athlete demonstrating hamstring tightness. The goal is 90 degrees.

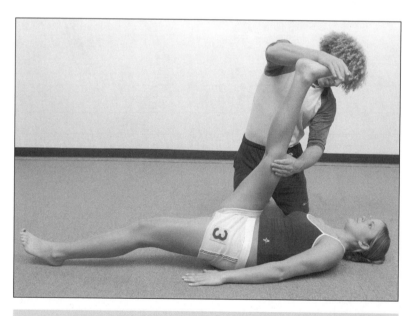

Figure 2.29 Athlete demonstrating excessive hamstring flexibility. This athlete may need to focus more on strengthening the hamstrings and less on flexibility.

Test

To assess hamstring flexibility, lie on your back and keep one leg straight with the foot flexed (toes pointing straight up). A partner should hold your other leg by the ankle. Keep the leg straight and raise it up until some slight resistance (muscle tightness) is felt. The goal is to maintain a straight leg and achieve a 90-degree angle. Failure to achieve this 90-degree angle means you need to perform some extra stretching for this area (figure 2.28). A tight hamstring (less than 90-degree angle) decreases your stride length when running. Because of its attachment to the pelvis, it can also affect alignment, which places more stress at the knee.

If you can go past 120 degrees, your hamstrings may be too flexible, and again you run the risk of the muscle not being strong enough for running and jumping (figure 2.29). An overly flexible hamstring may be weak, and this would destabilize the knee due to its inability to control the shear forces on the shinbone (tibia).

Corrective Stretch for Tight Hamstrings

To stretch the hamstring, sit on the floor or a table and stretch one leg out in front of you. The leg should be straight with the foot flexed. The other leg is in front with the knee bent and the foot in toward the groin. The key to this stretch is to keep the lower back straight and to reach forward with the chest (figure 2.30). If you reach with your hands, this will cause rounding of the upper back and a less effective stretch. Hold this stretch for 30 seconds, and repeat twice on each leg.

Figure 2.30 Corrective stretch for hamstring tightness. Notice how the athlete keeps her back straight and leads with her chest as she moves forward to stretch her hamstrings.

Area 5: Hip Flexors

The hip flexor region is an area that is commonly tight in athletes. Tightness in this area can shorten stride length during running. Decreased flexibility also places additional stress on the kneecap and reduces the strength of the side hip muscles. Remember that whenever you have tightness in one muscle group, you will often have weakness in a neighboring group. Athletes with tight hip flexors often have weakness in their side hip muscles.

Test

To assess flexibility of the hip flexor region, lie back on a table or end of a bench. Pull both knees up to your chest. Place both hands on one knee and slowly lower the opposite leg toward the ground so that it hangs down and not out to the side. Your thigh should be parallel with the ground. If it's not (figure 2.31), then you are too tight in the hip flexor region and will need to perform some corrective stretches. If your leg falls straight down and hangs below parallel, you may be overly flexible in this region and will need to perform some specific strengthening exercises.

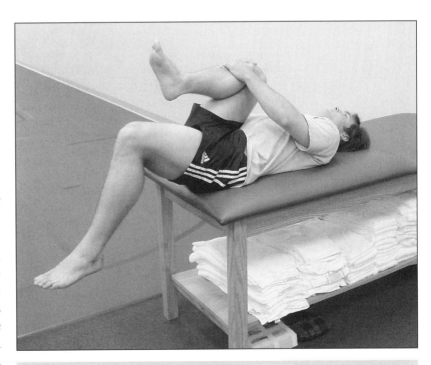

Figure 2.31 Hip flexor flexibility assessment. The thigh should hang parallel with the floor and the lower leg should hang straight down.

Figure 2.32 Corrective stretch for hip flexor tightness.

Corrective Stretch for Hip Flexor Tightness

To stretch the hip flexors, kneel down on one knee with one leg straight out behind you and the other leg bent and out in front. While keeping your upper body "tall," slowly slide your entire body forward until a stretch is felt in front of the hip and thigh (figure 2.32). Next, raise both arms straight over your head and turn your upper body opposite of the knee you have down (if your right knee is down, turn your upper body to the left). Hold for 30 seconds and repeat twice on each leg.

Area 6: Iliotibial Band

The iliotibial band (ITB) originates from the outside of the hip and travels down the leg to insert just below the knee. The ITB runs fibers to the outside of the kneecap. Because of this attachment, tightness will place extra pressure on the kneecap and contribute to dislocations of the kneecap. Tightness will also limit the leg's ability to turn inward during cutting maneuvers and thus place more stress on the knee.

Test

To test for tightness of the ITB, you can perform the following two tests. The first is the same test used to assess the hip flexor region. As you lower your leg, if your leg wants to fall out to the side, then you have some ITB tightness (figure 2.33). A second test involves lying on your back in a sit-up position. With your arms out to the side or on your chest, slowly roll your knees to one side, and as your knees approach the ground, position one foot on top of the other. Your knees should easily touch, and failure to do so is a second indicator of tightness in the ITB region (figure 2.34).

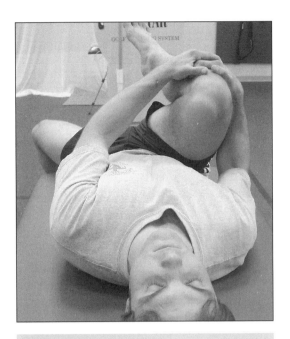

Figure 2.33 Top view of the same test used to assess tightness of the hip flexors. Notice how the left leg hangs out to the side. This would indicate iliotibial band (ITB) tightness.

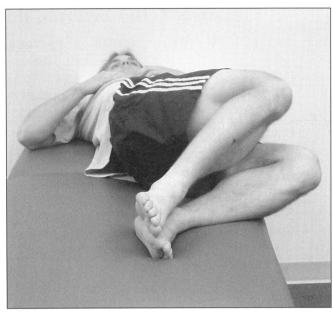

Figure 2.34 Failure to perform a roll to the side and have the knees touch in a relaxed position would also indicate tightness in the ITB region.

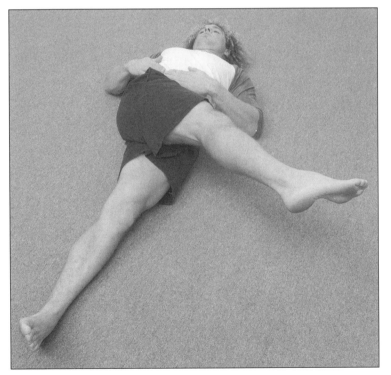

Figure 2.35 Corrective stretch for ITB tightness. Make sure to let the leg turn inward as it falls toward the ground.

Corrective Stretch for ITB Tightness

To stretch the ITB area, you will need to lie on your back. Lift one leg, and while keeping it straight, slowly lower the leg across your body. As the leg is lowered gradually, turn the leg and foot inward to increase the stretch (figure 2.35). Hold for 30 seconds and repeat two times on each side.

Area 7: Hip External Rotators

Hip rotator muscles are the muscles on the side of the hips. They are commonly tight in athletes. These small muscles help give stability to the hip, aid in balance, and help control rotational forces throughout the entire leg. Adequate strength and flexibility in these muscles will allow you to move more quickly from side to side and have more explosion with your first step.

Test

To test for tightness, lie on your back with your knees bent. Pull one knee up toward its opposite shoulder (figure 2.36). You should be able to bring your knee toward the opposite shoulder and over your chest. Failure to do this would indicate excessive tightness in the hip external rotators. If you can pull your knee all the way to your shoulder, you may have too much flexibility and may need to focus more on strengthening your hips (see the exercises in chapter 3 and in the overload sections of the Jumpmetrics workout plans).

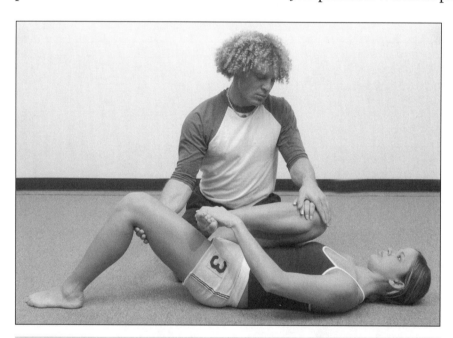

Figure 2.36 Hip external rotator assessment. This athlete can almost take her knee and place it on her shoulder. She may need to focus more on strength than flexibility.

Corrective Stretch for Tightness of the Hip External Rotators

The stretch to correct tightness of the external rotators is the same as the test. Simply hold the end of the test position for 30 seconds and repeat two times on each side.

Area 8: Hip Internal Rotators

The hip internal rotators are also often overlooked in athletes. Tightness in this area limits the hip motion necessary to squat and cut properly.

Test

To test flexibility of this region, you will need a partner to assist you. Lie on your back with your legs straight and toes pointed toward the ceiling. While you keep one leg straight, the partner lifts your other leg, allowing the knee to bend to a right angle (figure 2.37a). While maintaining this right angle, your partner will passively rotate your foot and lower leg outward. Your hip should turn out to form a 45-degree angle (figure 2.37b). Failure to turn out 45 degrees is an indicator that you have hip internal rotator tightness and will need to perform some corrective stretches. If your foot and lower leg rotate outward greater than 45 degrees, you may have excessive flexibility in this region, and you will need to focus additional time on hip strengthening (see the exercises in chapter 3 and in the overload sections of the Jumpmetrics workout plans).

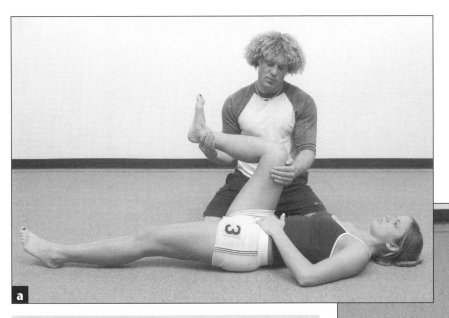

Figure 2.37 *(a)* Hip internal rotator assessment. The leg should turn out 45 degrees. *(b)* Close-up of hip internal rotator assessment. Notice how far the leg can be turned out before resistance is felt.

Corrective Stretch for Tightness of the Hip Internal Rotators

Lie on your back and stretch one leg so that the knee is bent to 90 degrees and approximately one foot away from the body's midline (figure 2.38a). Gently let that knee fall inward to feel a stretch in the front or back of the hip (figure 2.38b). You should feel this stretch the hip region slightly. The keys to this stretch are to keep your knee bent to 90 degrees and to make sure you don't feel the stretch on the inside of the knee. If you feel the stretch on the inside of the knee, check the angle of your knee (to make sure a 90-degree angle is maintained) and lessen the intensity of the stretch.

Figure 2.38 *(a)* Start position for corrective stretch for tightness of hip internal rotators. *(b)* End position for corrective stretch for tightness of hip internal rotators.

Area 9: Shoulders and Upper Back

The upper body is seldom checked for flexibility in athletes unless they are swimmers or baseball pitchers. Upper body flexibility can be very important for other athletes as well, such as soccer players and basketball players. Having decreased flexibility in your shoulders and upper back will affect your running posture, defensive stance, and ability to reach overhead.

Test

To test for tightness in your shoulders and upper back, lie on the floor (face-down) and grab a dowel overhead. Place your forehead on the ground and straighten your elbows completely to grasp the dowel with your arms approximately shoulder-width apart. While keeping your wrists in a neutral position, raise the dowel off the ground (figure 2.39). With your elbows straight, you should be able to raise the dowel 12 inches off the ground. Failure to do this would indicate tightness, and a corrective stretching regimen would need to be implemented.

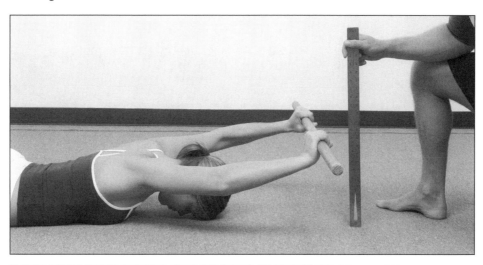

Figure 2.39   Assessment of shoulder and upper back flexibility.

Corrective Stretch for Tightness in the Shoulders and Upper Back

Lean against a table or the edge of a bed with your elbows together and your hips going toward your heels. Let your upper back relax and "sag" (figure 2.40a). You should feel the stretch in your upper back or latissimus region. You should not feel any discomfort in your shoulders. After holding the "sag" position for 30 seconds, round your upper back to increase the stretch felt in the latissimus region (figure 2.40b). Repeat twice for each stretch. Measure your shoulder flexibility weekly if you did not achieve 12 inches on the test.

Flexibility is sometimes neglected in the athlete's workout regimen. By taking these tests, you can see which areas you need to work on and which areas may be overly flexible. Overflexibility can be a big problem if an area is weak, so make sure you are performing the correct resistance exercises to strengthen these areas (see the exercises in chapter 3 and in the overload sections of the Jumpmetrics workout plans). Attention to proper flexibility will ensure that you can work out harder, recover quicker, and reach your full athletic potential.

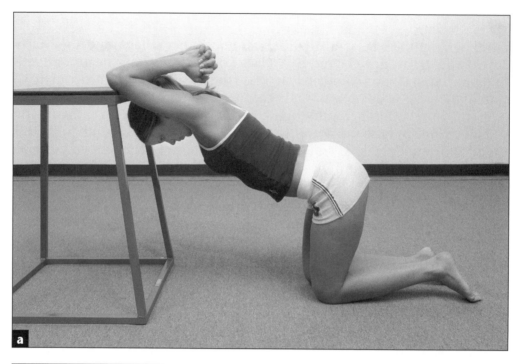

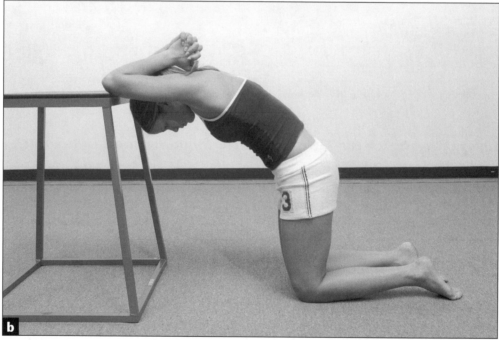

Figure 2.40 *(a)* "Prayer stretch" with back sagging to stretch the upper back and latissimus region of the upper body. *(b)* "Prayer stretch" with back rounded to stretch the latissimus region of the upper body and increase shoulder range of motion.

3

Developing High-Powered Hips

One of the biggest deficits seen in athletes today is weakness in their hips. To see the muscles we are talking about, refer to figure 3.1 on page 40. Athletes tend to be strong in the hip flexors and gluteus maximus but often have deficits in the hip abductor region. These deficits cause athletes to lose control of their knees during jumping and cutting. This lack of control can cause performance to suffer drastically. This chapter will show you how to strengthen and train this often neglected area. Doing so will improve your side-to-side quickness. In addition, strengthening these muscles will improve your balance and increase your power.

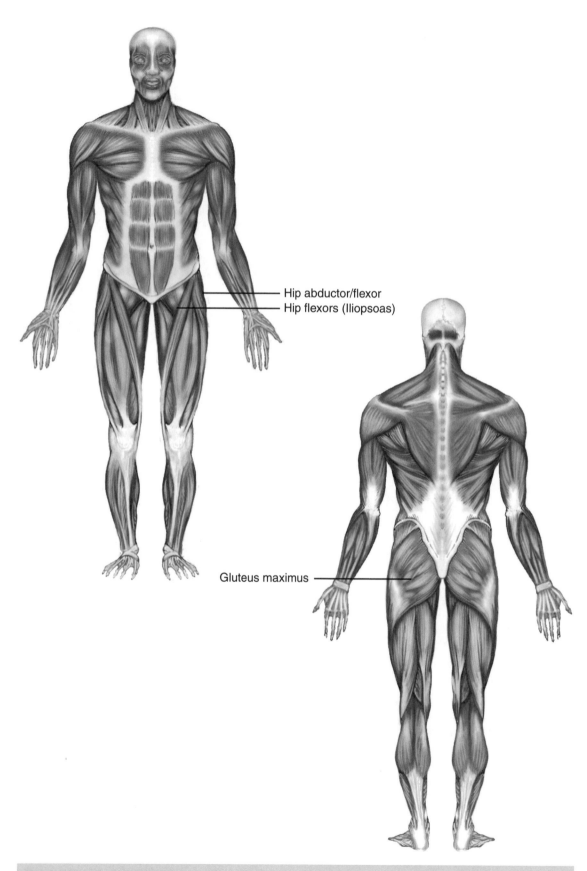

Hip abductor/flexor
Hip flexors (Iliopsoas)

Gluteus maximus

Figure 3.1 Muscle groups important to the strength of the hips.

Area 1: Gluteals

The gluteals are the muscles commonly known as the "butt" muscles. Take the following test to see if you have enough endurance in these muscles to allow you to achieve the optimal training level. (This test is an excellent drill for gauging players at the start of a preseason training program.)

Assume a "defensive position" with your body appropriately hinged at your hips and your back straight. Your feet will be approximately shoulder-width apart. Once you achieve this position, squat down so that you form a 90-degree angle at the knee. You should be able to hold this position for three minutes. If you feel this exercise only in your thighs (quadriceps), check your form and make sure your knees are not in front of your toes. If you do not feel this exercise work your "buttocks" region, then you have overdominant quadriceps (thighs), and you will benefit greatly from this chapter.

The exercises in this section do not involve the use of exercise machines; therefore, you can always work on balance. Including balance training in your workout regimen will also strengthen the side hip muscles (hip abductors), and this will help with your running, cutting, and jumping capabilities.

Squats With Dumbbells

Use the defensive position shown above to perform this exercise. Hold a pair of dumbbells with your hands up toward your shoulders and your elbows tucked in by your sides. Next perform a squat to achieve a good defensive position. Remember, you should achieve this same defensive position each time you squat to help train your muscles to remember a good position. Make sure to keep your back straight (not rounded) when fully down in the squat position. You should never feel this exercise work your back or your kneecap region. If you do, you should have someone check your form because you may be rounded or your knees may be forward over your toes.

Single-Leg Squats

There are several versions of the single-leg squat. The following versions of the exercise are included at different locations within the Jumpmetrics workout plan. The single-leg squat is also performed during the Jumpmetrics screening in chapter 2. Practice this squat regularly to strengthen your lower body.

One-Leg Squat With Ankle Tuck

Start in a standing position. Tuck one foot tightly behind the ankle of the support leg. Extend both arms in front of you at shoulder height, and stick your buttocks back to initiate the squat motion. Squat and try to achieve a 90-degree angle with the upper thigh and the lower leg before returning to the upright position. Keep your back straight. You may need to place a chair behind you the first few repetitions so you can learn how to squat properly.

One-Leg Squat With Leg Out Front

Standing on one leg, perform a squat. In the learning stage of the exercise, you can hold on to a stable object for support. As you reach a more advanced stage, this exercise can be performed with no support. The free leg and arms are held out in front of the body, and the support leg performs a squat until the buttock is close to the heel on the support foot. The foot of the support leg should always remain flat on the floor. The knee on the support leg should always be kept behind the toe by pushing the buttocks back to a point well behind the heel. At complete extension, the athlete can jump from the ground to increase the intensity of the exercise.

One-Leg Squat With Weight Vest

Perform any version of the single-leg squat while wearing a weight vest to increase resistance.

Alternating Leg Lunge

From a standing position, step with one leg out to the front of the body. Allow the leg to bend at the knee, lowering the body toward the floor. Allow the back leg to bend when first learning the exercise. As you become more advanced, keep the back leg straight, forcing the front leg to step out from the standing position even farther. To finish, push back to a standing position off the front leg. Alternate legs throughout the exercise. This exercise can also be done walking from one point to another.

Variation: When you step out from the standing position, keep the leg out front, and straighten it and bend it three times before pushing yourself back to a standing position. This pumping of the leg will emphasize the level of muscle fatigue, which is the objective in phase one.

Transverse or Rotational Lunge

To work the hip and thigh muscles in a rotational manner, perform a lunge to the side, allowing the lead leg to rotate and strike the ground with the toes pointing in the direction of the stride. Rotating the lead leg will cause the muscles of the inner thigh to stabilize and strengthen. The lead knee should not extend in front of the toes, and the toes should point forward. The trail leg should remain straight, and the foot should remain as it was in the start position. Your arms are extended in front of the body, and the torso is turned forward and faces the same direction as the toes.

Baby Squats

Perform short-range (i.e., baby) squats in a shallow or deep range. Perform the exercise slowly or quickly for a specified time or number of reps.

Static Squat

Perform a squat by flexing the knees, hips, and ankles to either a three-quarter or one-half squat position (see photo at right). Hold the posture for an assigned amount of time.

One-Leg Squat With Jump

Perform a one-leg squat (using a chair for support). As you complete the movement, jump from the ground. The free leg should be held with the upper thigh parallel to the floor and the foot clear of the ground.

One-Leg Romanian Dead Lift

Standing on one leg, bend forward at the waist. As the upper body bends forward, keep the support leg slightly bent. At the same time, allow the free leg to come up behind you. Bend forward toward the floor or the foot of the support leg, and then return to the starting position (keeping the free leg from touching the floor throughout the exercise). Once upright, allow the knee of the support leg to bend four to five inches, thus moving into a partial squat. After squatting, return to the standing position to complete the repetition. Perform a specified number of repetitions on one leg before switching.

Around the World (Circuit)

This is a leg circuit consisting of a combination of body weight leg exercises, such as squat and lunge variations and step slides, that can be performed in any formation (e.g., around a basketball court or across a field). On a basketball court, begin by performing 10 squats in the corner of the court. After performing the squats, do lunges down the length of the floor. Perform 10 squats in the next corner. Next perform a step slide exercise across the baseline of the court. Perform 10 squats in the next corner, followed again by lunges down the length of the floor. Complete the circuit by performing 10 squats again in the final corner, followed by another set of step slides across the opposite baseline. Any combination of body weight exercises can be used during this circuit. Jump squats (page 45) can be substituted for baby squats (page 44) and musketeer lunges (page 48) for step slides (page 118).

Lateral Lunge

To work the gluteus maximus and side hip muscles, perform a side or lateral lunge. Make sure that your knee does not bend past your toes. At the low position (with knee bent), make sure your hip, knee, and foot are in good alignment. The extended leg should remain straight, and you should allow the bent leg to roll in.

Slide Board

You need a high-quality slide board for this exercise. Sliding from side to side, allow the lead arm to swing out. Push off the trailing leg to begin the slide, and allow the lead leg to step in the direction you wish to slide to increase the effectiveness of the movement.

Backward Lunge

Adequate balance and core strength are the keys to performing this exercise. Extend your right leg behind you. Once the right foot hits the ground, allow the right knee to bend and almost touch the ground. In this "down" position, your left knee will also be bent. From that position (and keeping your trunk upright), push back with your left leg to stand up and bring your left foot equal to your right. If you do not have good balance or adequate core strength, you will not be able to keep your trunk in an upright position as you push back. Keep your spine slanted slightly forward as your leg goes behind you. Do not allow your body to lean backward as you push up to return to an upright position.

Musketeer Lunge

From a standing position, pull the left leg behind the right leg as if you were performing a carioca or grapevine maneuver. The right leg becomes the supporting leg. Allow the front leg (right leg) to bend at the knee, lowering the body toward the floor. Keep the back leg as straight as possible. Push the right leg back up to a standing position, while at the same time bringing the left leg beside the right to finish the repetition. Alternate the leg that steps behind during the exercise. This exercise can also be done walking sideways from one point to another. When doing this, the same leg always steps behind; you can then walk back to the starting point by stepping behind with the opposite leg.

Musketeer Lunge With Side Kick

From a standing position, step the right leg behind the left leg as if you were performing a carioca or grapevine maneuver. The left leg becomes the supporting leg. Allow the left leg to bend at the knee, lowering the body toward the floor. Keep the right leg (the back leg) as straight as possible. Fully extend the left leg to return to a standing position, while at the same time bringing the right leg beside the left and then up to the chest with the knee bent. Slowly extend the right leg out to the side in a controlled kicking motion. Keep the foot turned sideways and parallel to the floor. After the designated number of repetitions, repeat the exercise with the other leg. This exercise can also be done walking sideways from one point to another. When doing this, the same leg always steps behind.

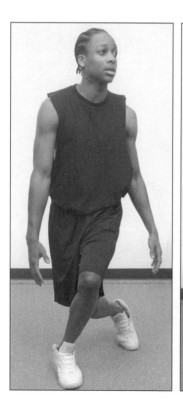

Area 2: Hip Abductors

The hip abductors are the muscles on the side of your hips. This is an area that is commonly weak among athletes. The hip abductors control rotation in the lower extremity, and strengthening these muscles will allow you to move quicker from side to side and to cut more sharply. Take the following test to see if you have baseline strength in the hip abductor region.

Lie on your side with both legs straight. Make sure your body is in a perfectly straight line. Bring the bottom knee up toward your chest to form a right angle with your knee. Now, raise the upper leg (keeping it straight) so that it is slightly above parallel with the ground, and move the leg slightly behind you to isolate the side hip muscles (*a*). Slowly raise the leg up and down for 30 seconds. At the end of the 30 seconds, hold the leg in the up position and turn the leg in and out while maintaining a body that is perfectly straight (*b-c*). You will perform this rotational movement for a total of 30 seconds. Finally, after this 30-second interval, keep the leg in the up position and bend your knee back and forth for 30 seconds as if performing a hamstring curl on your side (*d*). This 90-second test is very difficult for many athletes and gives them a good indication that they can use some work in this region.

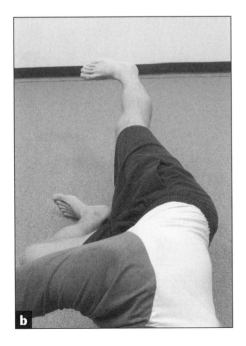
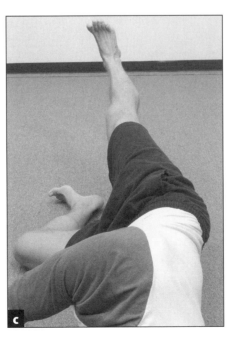

To address deficits in this region, perform the following two hip training circuits. Remember that a circuit is a continuous loop, so you will perform these exercises one after the other with no rest time in between. Increased endurance is the main goal with these circuits.

Hip Circuit #1

Hip Flex

While standing in place, lift one leg as high as you can, bringing the knee as close to the chest as possible without bending the back forward. To complete the movement, lower the leg to where the foot is six to eight inches from the ground. Perform all the movements on one leg at a time.

Donkey Kick

Kneeling on your hands and knees, kick one leg back until it is perfectly straight behind you. The foot should be held in dorsiflexion (toe toward shin) as if to put your foot flat on the wall behind you. To complete the movement, bring the knee of the extended leg as close to the chest as possible. Perform all the movements on one leg at a time.

Fire Hydrant

Kneeling on your hands and knees, lift one knee up to the side. Attempt to keep the foot and leg all at the same level. Return the knee to the floor to complete the movement.

Kick the Hydrant

Kneeling on your hands and knees, lift one knee up to the side. Attempt to keep the foot and leg all at the same level. Kick the leg out to the side so that the leg and the body form an L. Pull the knee back to its prekick position, and then return the knee to the floor to complete the movement.

Hip Circuit #2

Single-Leg Balance Reach to the Floor

Balance on one leg, and while maintaining your balance, bend at your hip to reach down to the floor. Once you touch the floor, return to the starting position, maintaining your balance throughout the exercise. Make sure you bend at your hips and keep your back straight as you reach down toward the floor. To increase the intensity of the exercise, stand on an apparatus that challenges your balance and perform the same balance reach to the floor.

Standing Hip Rotation

While standing, raise one knee so that your thigh is parallel with the floor. Turn your body in the opposite direction of the knee that is raised (e.g., if you picked up your right knee, you will turn your body to the left). Keep turning as far as possible, trying not to lose your balance, and then return to the starting position.

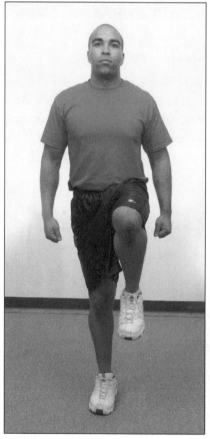

Standing Lateral Kicks

While standing, raise one knee so that your thigh is parallel with the floor. Kick the raised leg out to the side as if kicking someone in the chest. Only kick as high as you can without losing your balance. If you lose your balance, reduce the height of the kick until your balance improves. Return to the start position after each kick and try not to put your foot down. Try to kick with your heel because this will cause more stretch to occur throughout your muscles.

(end Hip Circuit #2)

Slow Low Step Slide With Ankle Tether

Assume a good defensive position and place a band around your ankles so that the band has some slight tension. While maintaining this tension and a good defensive position, take a step to the side with your left foot, and then bring your right foot in toward your left foot to return to a good defensive position. Keep leading with your left foot, always keeping tension on the cord. You should not feel this exercise work your back. If you do, then you are not in a good defensive position. You should feel this exercise work the side hip muscles. You can also perform the exercise for a certain distance, making sure each leg gets a chance to lead the slide motion.

Tether With Internal Lunge

Place a tether cord around your ankles. Begin the movement by stepping out with the front leg and rotating the foot externally (away from the centerline of the body). The front foot should end firmly on the ground with the foot pointing in the direction you are moving. Then move the back leg slightly toward the front leg. The tension on the tether should always keep the center of the cord from sagging toward the floor. This exercise will strengthen the external rotators of the hips.

Lateral Unders

Perform a side lunge so that your body and head move laterally under a hurdle (see figure below). To emphasize the groin and hamstring stretch, attempt to keep the foot of the extended leg flat on the floor. As you come out from under the hurdle, return to a full standing position.

Step Overs

Perform a lateral under, but as you come out from under the hurdle, bring your knee up high, and step back over the hurdle in the direction you just came from with the leg closest to the hurdle. After all assigned repetitions on one side are complete, the hurdle should be approached from the opposite direction.

Area 3: Trunk

If you had trouble with test 7 (pelvis lift/bridge) in chapter 2, this section is for you. This section will focus on the gluteals and how these muscles, along with the smaller back muscles of the spine, help control rotational forces in the spine. Many times athletes will have strength in their hips but still not have good control of the rotation in the spine. This lack of control can decrease their cutting and jumping ability as well as place more stress on their knees. Repeat test 7 from chapter 2 to reevaluate whether you have adequate rotational control of your trunk.

Lie on the ground in a bridge position. Keeping your feet on the ground and arms across your chest, lift your hips up. Stop raising once your knees, hips, and shoulders make one line. While maintaining this position, focus on keeping your hips level and not letting them drop or tilt from side to side. Lift one knee and foot approximately three to four inches, and see what happens to the pelvis. In the efficient state, the pelvis should remain level, and you should not feel the exercise work the lower back muscles. The inability to keep your pelvis level when raising one leg means you are not as efficient through the core as you need to be, and this will lessen your ability to train effectively. To help train this area, perform the following exercises.

One-Leg Bridge With Foot on Floor

Lie on your back in a bridge position by bending your knees and placing your foot on the floor just away from your buttocks. Lift and straighten one knee so that your thighs remain level. Your arms will be down by your side. Tighten your abdominal muscles and then raise your hips. Try to raise your hips high enough to create a line between your knees, hips, and shoulders. Your hips should remain level at all times. Start with your arms by your side and progress to arms across your chest to make the exercise more difficult. Make sure you keep your thighs and pelvis level. You should never feel this exercise work your lower back. Once you are able to do 20 reps of this exercise, you can experiment with trying to do a single-leg bridge with your upper body on a foam roll or on a basketball, soccer ball, or medicine ball to increase the difficulty.

Single-Leg Bridge

Like the single-leg squat, the single-leg bridge is a variation of the pelvis lift (bridge) exercise performed during the Jumpmetrics screening in chapter 2. The following versions of the single-leg bridge are included at different locations within the Jumpmetrics workout plans. You should practice this skill in order to strengthen your body in the proper way.

Two-Leg Bridge With Feet on Big Ball

Another way to challenge your trunk muscles and rotational strength is to lie on the ground and place both feet on top of a "balance" ball. Place your arms by your sides and raise your hips as in the previous bridge exercises. Make sure your hips are high enough to bring them into alignment with your knees and shoulders. Hold the position, and while keeping your arms straight, alternately move your arms back and forth over your head. Only start moving your arms once you have reached your balance point on the ball. Make sure you do not feel the exercise work your lower back.

One-Leg Bridge on Big Ball

Lie down with your upper back on the ball. Your lower back and legs will be off the ball. Keep your hips up to create a straight and level line between your knees, hips, and shoulders. While your legs are out in front of you, practice lifting one knee and foot slightly off the ground without losing your balance. You can also try to straighten one knee at a time, trying to keep your pelvis level. Keep your hips up and focus on keeping your pelvis level as you straighten or lift one knee. Hold the end of the movement for a count of two.

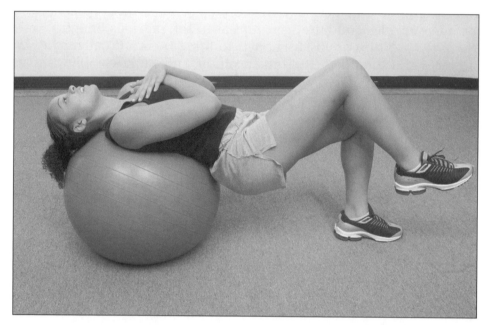

One-Leg Bridge With Foot on Big Ball

Once you can perform all the other balance ball exercises, you can then work on mastering this exercise. This exercise requires excellent strength and balance in the hips and low back muscles. Lying on the floor, put one foot on top of the ball and extend the other leg in the air. Position the thighs so they are even with each other, and while keeping the abdominal muscles tight, raise the pelvis. Raise the pelvis high enough so the knee, pelvis, and shoulder form a straight line. Hold

for a count of five. You should not feel the muscles work in your low back region. If you do, stop, retighten your abdominal muscles, and start again. If you continue to feel the exercise work your low back, it may be too advanced. Start with your arms on the floor for additional support. To make the exercise more difficult, cross your arms on your chest. This will decrease the base of support and make the exercise more challenging.

One-Leg Bridge With Foot on Medicine Ball

Lie on your back with a medicine ball beside your knees on the floor. Bend one of your knees and place your foot on the medicine ball. Keep the other leg straight and extended off the floor. While keeping your abdominal muscles and buttocks tight, raise your hips from the floor. Hold this position for a specified amount of time and then switch feet.

One-Leg Bridge With Hip Twist

Perform this exercise the same as the one-leg bridge with foot on big ball, except remove the ball from the exercise. While holding the position, allow the hips to twist slightly as if to push the hip toward the ceiling, and then return the hips to parallel. Repeat this twisting for a specified amount of time.

Bench Hamstrings

Lean the upper mid-back and shoulders against an exercise bench. Both feet are flat on the floor. Bring the hips up until the thighs, abdomen, and chest are parallel to the floor. Keep your arms crossed over your chest. Raise one foot from the floor and extend that leg, keeping the leg in line with the body. Then lower the hips to the floor, using the upper shoulders as a fulcrum. The buttock should touch the floor as close to the bench as possible. Return the hips to the starting position to complete the movement.

Bench Hamstrings With Foot on Balance Disc

Perform this exercise the same as the bench hamstrings, but place the foot of the support leg on a balance disc device to further challenge the hamstring.

Bench Hamstrings With Weight Vest

Perform this exercise the same as the bench hamstrings, but wear a weighted vest to add load to the movement.

Burpees

Begin in a standing position. Squat down with both knees bent and place both hands on the floor in front of your feet. Extend both legs back and assume a push-up position. Perform a push-up. Jump back into the squat, returning the feet back to their starting position beside your hands. Return to a standing position to complete the repetition.

Burpee/Squat Jump

Begin in a standing position. Squat down with both knees bent and place both hands on the floor in front of your feet. Extend both legs back and assume a push-up position. Perform a push-up. Return to the squat and jump into the air by fully extending the knees, ankles, and hips (*a*). Fully extend your arms above your head. Land softly, first on the balls of the feet, and quickly transferring your weight to your heels (*b*). Bend the knees to absorb additional forces. Move directly into the next burpee to begin the next repetition.

Coordinating Your Newly Developed Strength

Having strength in the hips and core is essential for increased sports performance. However, strength is only beneficial to you if you have the ability to get those strong muscles to work at the proper time and in the proper sequence. Even if the muscles are strong, if they fail to work in a coordinated manner, that strength is wasted. Along with your strength training, it is important to work the muscles at higher speeds and with predictable and unpredictable changes of direction. The following drills are located in the "Power" section of the Jumpmetrics workout plans. In the Jumpmetrics plan, they are considered to be power exercises because of the muscular coordination and body position required to perform the drills correctly. If you assume the incorrect position by getting your feet too close to one another or by putting your body weight on the incorrect foot, you will struggle to regain your position and your power will be lost.

Cutting Consideration

There are really only a few foot and leg patterns an athlete uses to move during sporting activities. You will commonly see athletes perform three essential steps in order to make a play. These steps are the jab step, drop step, and crossover step. Although your body's movement abilities limit you to just these three steps, the combinations of the three can be very confusing for someone trying to defend your advancement.

When doing change of direction drills, it's important to consider how you will manage your movements. You will normally (a) move to and from an object or other player, (b) shadow or defend another player, or (c) cut around an object or player in order to get somewhere. These tasks require movement skills.

Moving Productively To and From an Object

When you move toward an object but realize that you have misjudged the play, or you need to change direction rapidly, it is best to plant the foot farthest from the object firmly, placing nearly all your body weight on this *plant leg*. The leg closest to the person or object, called the *tag leg*, should have very little of the body's weight applied to it. This shift in body weight to the plant leg helps to avoid a load force on the tag leg while twisting on it. Move the arms aggressively to help provide counterlift and acceleration. These upper and lower body techniques will improve performance as well as help to avoid injury.

Moving Productively Around an Object

As an athlete moves toward and around an object or opponent, the athlete should consider the most effective way to circle while still maintaining high speed. The fastest way to go around an opponent or object is by leaning into the object as close as possible with the nearest shoulder. Also, the near foot should step around the object in an attempt to position the toe in the direction the athlete plans to go. Once the near shoulder clears the object, the athlete should move the arms aggressively to help provide counterlift and acceleration.

Cutting on the inside leg does present risk because of the greater muscular force required to control the higher degree of angular acceleration. If the muscles are weak, injury potential may be greater while cutting on the inside leg. Practicing the technique in slowly increased speed intervals, along with constructive strengthening exercise, will enhance the ability of the muscle to perform over time.

The question many may ask is, Why perform a higher-risk movement at all when you can opt for the lower-risk technique? Intuitively, the athlete will choose to perform in a way that provides the highest performance regardless of the long-term effects. During training, if you do not address the technique that athletes commonly use during play, injury will likely occur during a game as a result of poor preparation. Remember that a strength and conditioning plan should, at some point, require you to perform with loads and techniques that mimic a level more difficult than actual play; playing the sport will then seem easy by comparison.

Three-Cone Reaction

Stand about five yards from three cones placed in a straight line about five yards apart from one another. The cones are assigned a number from left to right of 1, 2, and 3. The starting position is called *back*. A partner (coach or teammate) instructs you to move to the cones by calling out a number, or instructs you to return to the starting position by calling out, "Back." The partner can instruct you to move from cone to cone, or from the *back* position to any cone.

Cone Pattern

Stand in front of a cone to use it as a positional reference point. Jab step (quick short step) with the left foot on the left side of the cone. As the left foot makes contact with the ground, the right foot should leave the ground slightly. Return to the starting position by returning the right foot to the ground and then the left foot to its starting point in front of the cone. Repeat the process to the right side of the cone, moving forward with the right foot in the lead. This is a 1-1, 2-1 pattern with the feet (i.e., left-right, left-right pattern). The drill can be altered by stepping to the left side of the cone with the right foot to form a crossover step move. The steps still follow the 1-1, 2-1 pattern in both movement patterns.

Box Reaction

Stand in the center of four cones placed in the shape of a square. The cones should be an equal distance of 10 yards apart from each other. A partner (coach) directs you to move either forward, backward, side to side, or diagonally, or the partner may instruct you to jump. Usually, 15 to 20 seconds of work should be allowed.

20-Yard Shuttle

Place two cones 10 yards apart. Mark a starting spot directly in the center between the cones. Begin the movement by assuming a crouched athletic position at the starting point. On command, stay low and turn and sprint to your right. You will sprint straight ahead, then turn around at the cone (cutting off the outside leg) and come back. As you approach the cone, plant your left leg and touch the line at the cone's front edge with your right hand. Your right leg will be the tag leg and will have to go slightly over the line to ensure that the hand has enough spacing to touch the line. The tag leg in this movement must remain non–weight bearing (the plant leg will spin and bear all of the weight of the turn). Once you touch the line, turn and sprint to the opposite cone. The *right leg* becomes the plant leg, and the *left leg* becomes the tag leg. The left hand will touch the line at the left cone's edge. After touching the line, turn and sprint to the starting point to complete the movement. Always attempt to keep your body leaning toward the opposite cone as you cut. This will ensure a proper lean in the intended direction of the next sprint.

Cone Ladder

Place a series of cones in a straight line approximately three feet apart from one another. There are two versions of this drill:

• The side-to-side version of the drill is done totally with the step slide exercise. Rapidly step slide to the next cone in line and then back to the starting cone. Repeat the pattern, progressing to each cone in the line, always returning to the starting cone. You should keep the tag foot (the foot moving toward the cone) very light on the change of direction. This is done by keeping the plant foot (the foot away from the cone) very heavy. This technique will ensure maximum speed in the movement.

• The forward and back version of the drill is done by sprinting forward to a cone and then backward to the start cone. Sprint to the first cone, then run backward quickly to the starting point; next sprint to the second cone, then run backward to the starting point, and so on. The cones are managed in the same way as the side-to-side version of the exercise. You should work the arms along with the legs (opposite arm to leg). On the backward run, the body should have an exaggerated forward lean to ensure proper balance. Choose one leg to be the forward plant leg and the opposite leg to be the backward plant leg. The forward and backward leg should stay the same throughout the drill (they can be switched for the next set of the drill). This assignment of legs is a great way to measure your distances on the movement and improve speed. When running backward, do not look for the cone over your shoulder; look straight ahead and train your peripheral vision to see the start cone as you come to it.

Sprint Cutting

Begin 20 to 30 yards from a partner (teammate or coach). On command, run toward a cone just in front of the partner. As you reach the cone, the partner gives you a left or right directional command. You then make a sharp cut to the left or right. You must be aware of which foot is the tag leg and which foot is the plant leg. In this case, the tag leg will be the leg away from the direction you intend to go. You should stay on the toe of the tag leg's foot during the cut to avoid placing too much twisting force (torque) on the joints. The amount of pressure on the tag leg should be as light as possible, creating a bouncing effect. This bounce will force you to rapidly shift weight to the plant leg (the leg toward the intended direction of the cut). The partner can ask you to jump vertically when you get to the cone as well.

Zigzag Run (Outside Leg)

Place two lines of cones 15 yards apart and diagonal to one another. Perform the drill by running diagonally across the court from cone to cone. Each time you reach one of the cones, cut back toward the opposite cone by using your outside leg.

Zigzag Run (Inside Leg)

A variation of the zigzag run drill is to perform your changes of direction off the inside leg. This will cause you to spin as you make your cut. Another variation is to cut off the outside leg at one cone, and then cut off the inside leg at the next cone. During this variation, the same leg will be doing the cutting each change of direction. In this variation, you must switch legs and repeat the drill. Complete three sets of 10 changes of direction with each leg.

Called Pattern Jumps

Numbers are presented in patterns on a stable surface (see photo at left). The coach calls the numbers out at random or assigns the entire pattern to be completed in sequence (1-10).

Hexagon Drill

Using tape or paint, create a hexagon (with two-foot sides) on the ground. Stand in the center of the hexagon and jump in and out of the shape on every side. Always return to the center of the hexagon. Complete three turns around the entire shape. The exercise should be timed. The time begins when you first jump out and then stops when you reenter the shape from the side adjacent to the side where you began.

4

Drills to Enhance Power

Along with its focus on proper technique and posture during athletic activities, the Jumpmetrics program is designed to help athletes increase performance in their sport. To become effective members of their team, most athletes must demonstrate the ability to move with power. An athlete's muscular power is commonly enhanced through activities that evoke the stretch-shortening cycle.

Stretch-Shortening Cycle

Afferent nerve fibers carry messages from the distant parts of the body to the spine and brain. *Efferent* fibers, on the other hand, send messages from the brain and spine back to the periphery. When a muscle is stretched, information is sent via the afferent (conducting) nerve fibers—namely, the muscle spindles—to the spinal cord. This information conveys an alert to the spinal cord regarding the muscle's potential to stretch too far. In response, the spinal cord rapidly returns neural (efferent) information to the muscle through the nerve fibers. This return message instructs the muscle to protectively contract to prevent overstretching that could lead to injury. This stretch-shortening cycle is an intrinsic reflex response that occurs any time a muscle is placed under tension. Even though sitting is not a highly athletic activity, the stretch-shortening cycle is helping you balance yourself and maintain your posture even while you sit and read this paragraph. As an athlete, it is important to optimize this reflex action. The more quickly afferent and efferent messages can be interchanged, the more rapid and forceful a muscle contraction can occur, thus promoting greater speed and power of movement.

Becoming Reactive

Explosive jumping ability, first-step quickness, and lateral speed are abilities that are based on the reactivity of muscle. When standing on a diving board, you can achieve greater takeoff height by causing the board to quickly bend farther. The same is true of muscle. However, in the case of muscle, it is not the firm ground or floor under your feet that will provide a pliable takeoff force; instead, it is the muscle that must act as the springboard. You can improve your muscles' springboard effect (power) by using both resistance training and specific power drills. The most important type of strength in regard to power development is *reactive strength*.

Reactive strength is improved by teaching the muscle to move more efficiently from a stretched position to an active position (eccentric to concentric muscle contractions). Rapidly crouching prior to accelerating upward during a jump stretches the muscles of the legs. This stretch acts like the diving board bending downward. The quicker this stretch occurs, the greater a force will be produced when the muscles attempt to reflexively shorten. This shortening (contraction) of the muscles acts like the diving board's rebound upward. The muscles' contraction will correspondingly slingshot you upward with greater force. So in a sense, if you use your muscles correctly, the diving board is within you.

Several training methods can be used to optimize the results of the stretch-shortening cycle. The stretch-shortening cycle can always be improved during resistance training. During the downward path of the squat exercise, for example, you must apply an eccentric muscle contraction in order to decelerate the weighted bar. At some point along the range of motion, you must upwardly accelerate the bar from the bottom of the squat position. If you can improve the skill of rapidly decelerating a movement, followed by acceleration, you will increase your muscle reactive ability.

Heavy resistance training exercises often move slowly. Therefore, this type of resistance training should be used to promote an environment of overload to the working muscles rather than overspeed. Overload training forces the muscle to adjust for load stresses greater than would commonly be encountered during the performance of the athlete's sport. By overloading the muscles, the athlete feels lighter when not overloaded and in normal performance.

A more athletically specific and highly reactive type of resistance training called *plyometrics* has recently become popular. The effects produced by plyometrics are similar to those of heavy resistance training, but plyometric movements result in visibly greater limb speeds. Plyometrics causes the athlete to coordinate contracting muscles in an overspeed environment similar to the speed required for sports play.

When both overspeed and overload training methods are incorporated into the workout program, neural improvements are made in *intramuscular* and *intermuscular* coordination (figure 4.1). Intramuscular coordination refers to how effectively actions occur *within* the muscle (e.g., neural communication, cross-bridging of muscle fiber, and chemical exchanges). Intermuscular coordination refers to the coordinated actions that occur *between* separate muscles or muscle groups.

The Jumpmetrics program uses both plyometric and heavy resistance training to contribute to power and speed development and to ensure that the athlete has full command of the muscles' abilities during both overspeed and

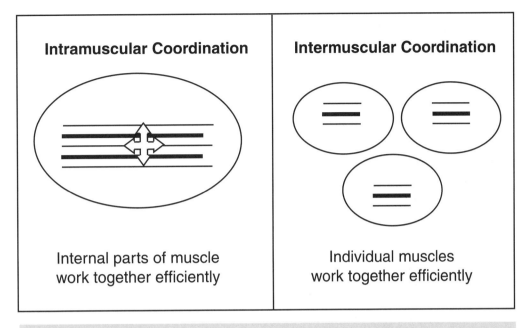

Figure 4.1 Illustration of intramuscular vs. intermuscular coordination.

overload conditions. Neither training method is better than the other. By employing both methods, you will produce the greatest gains. For example, to enhance jumping ability, you can perform a traditional squat exercise with very heavy resistance. The squatting movement may seem slow, but motor neurons must fire very rapidly to recruit a sufficient number of muscle fibers to control and move the weight. Squatting, however, does not involve the ankle or arm movements used during jumping. If your knee incorrectly moves over your toes during the squat, you will place additional stretch on the muscles of the calf (ankle); otherwise, the dorsiflexion of your foot should be minimal. The ankle action left out of squatting is plantar flexion (pointing the toe). To make this happen smoothly at high speed, you have to practice the plantar action. You can do this using plyometric jumping exercises. Failure to practice the plantar action will reduce efficiency of movement and reduce power in the lower leg. There is a lot of impact with squatting from the top down. That's where the benefit of squatting comes in—through overload. Jumping is a more athletic activity, and it requires coordination of all joint segments moving through their full ranges at the same time. Therefore, squatting is an excellent *intramuscular* exercise, while the high-speed act of jumping during plyometric training is an excellent *intermuscular* exercise.

An athlete's genetic potential plays a large role in how quickly information is transferred and how forcefully a muscle contracts. If you're lucky, your parents gave you many fast motor neurons (nerve cells), which give rise to a great number of fast-twitch muscle fibers (forcefully contracting muscle cells). However, there is no true way to measure your exact genetic poten-tial—all you can do is work out intelligently to ensure that your potential is optimized. Over the years, there have probably been many potential Michael Jordans, but only one has maximized his full potential.

The Jumpmetrics Plyometric Plan

Jumpmetrics incorporates plyometric movements into its routines to help athletes increase their power and speed and to help them develop more reactive muscles. Jumpmetrics uses plyometrics to teach the athlete proper joint position during high-speed, loaded movements (e.g., jumping and landing while doing a header in soccer or changing directions while running a pass route in football). Athletic injuries often occur during high-speed movements, in areas with surface instability, or when an athlete is physically inexperienced. Surface instability refers to uneven surfaces or slick playing areas where friction is decreased because of wet conditions. Inexperience causes uncertainty and slow athletic response processes. If someone is physically inexperienced, or if the playing conditions are unfamiliar, a loss of intramuscular or intermuscular coordination can result in injury-causing movement decisions. The Jumpmetrics plan makes proper form and position the first concern, and distance and height are the secondary goal.

The Jumpmetrics plan only includes a small number of plyometric activities. The quality of a movement is more important than the quantity of activities. The athleticism and body awareness gained from the training will help you avoid potentially dangerous postures and injury-causing situations.

As with any plyometric plan, if plyometric movements are performed too often, or performed on too hard a surface, overtraining of the nervous system can occur. The muscular system is much more resilient than the nervous system. As a result, the stress responses that commonly occur with overtraining are caused by the body's inability to regenerate neurotransmitters fast enough to maintain the function of the body systems (muscular system, immune system, endocrine system, and so on). Overtraining can result in poor performance. Keep in mind that the acceleration and deceleration techniques used in plyometric training are also applied during every other exercise within the Jumpmetrics training program. So it makes very little sense to be involved in an overly strenuous jump routine. In highly plyometric sports like basketball and volleyball, which are played on extremely hard surfaces, a little plyometric exercise goes a long way toward helping you improve.

Athletes who scored poorly on the Jumpmetrics evaluation (chapter 2, page 24) may be athletically inexperienced or physically immature. For these athletes, the plyometric exercises may need to be reduced in volume, performed on softer surfaces, or performed off two feet instead of one. Depending on your evaluation score, your Jumpmetrics routine will be structured to help you achieve the optimal results. Some plyometric exercises are easier on the body than others. Less complex exercises are used at the introductory level of plyometric training. These same exercises can be incorporated into the advanced athlete's training program as a means of providing a lower-stress training day.

Because plyometric exercise can be stressful to the body, Jumpmetrics is structured in such a way to minimize training stress. The plan uses systematic increases in workload to slowly increase the intensity of plyometric exercise at each training level. Periodization of overload training is also considered. Periodization reduces overwork stress through planned reductions in training intensity, with both lower-intensity training days and higher-intensity training days occurring during the same training week.

The Jumpmetrics plan has an established plyometric routine, but its plyometric foundation is based on two very simple concepts:

1. As the exercise becomes more intense, perform fewer sets of that exercise.
2. If the exercise is less intense, you can perform more sets of that exercise.

Approaching any exercise format with these rules in mind will prevent overwork and training-related injury.

Are You Physically Ready to Begin Plyometric Training?

Not all athletes are physically prepared for the same levels of plyometric training. Muscle weakness is a primary cause of injury. Several methods of strength assessment have been suggested as benchmark measurements for the plyometric novice. Soviet coaches, who originally developed plyometric training, suggest the ability to perform a single repetition maximum (1RM) squat with a weight one and a half to two times the athlete's body weight as the requirement for beginning the training. In the Jumpmetrics plan, a more pragmatic approach is taken to strength testing that can be applied to large groups of athletes at any age. To determine neuromuscular control and strength, the Jumpmetrics evaluation requires the athlete to perform three to four repetitions of a 90-degree one-legged squat while maintaining a proper position. When athletes perform their sports skills, they are often on one leg at a time. Testing the athlete on one leg should therefore be the standard for plyometric readiness.

In the Jumpmetrics plan, the plyometric training is structured based on the considerations for plyometric exercise suggested by the National Strength and Conditioning Association:

1. Keep exercises used during training specific to your sports activities.
2. Use low-intensity plyometric exercises in the early training period. Increase the intensity as the training progresses and before the sport season begins to ensure peak muscular power output.
3. As the intensity of exercise increases, decrease the volume (sets and reps) of training.
4. If you increase the intensity of the workouts, allow more recovery time between workouts.
5. Terminate the exercise when fatigue begins to occur and you can no longer perform the exercise correctly.
6. As the exercises become more difficult and complex due to agility and coordination requirements, reduce the number of sets and repetitions of that exercise.
7. During early training or athletic development, use low movement complexity. As you advance, use higher movement complexity.
8. Prior to the sport season, you can participate in more plyometric activity during the training week (not to exceed three plyometric training days). As the sport season approaches, the number of training sessions are reduced. During the in-season period, plyometric training should be used when you need it.

9. Keep the progression in plyometric training intensity slow. More is not necessarily better. A conservative approach to training is always advised. The SAID principle (specific adaptations to imposing demands) means that you should allow your body to adapt to the exercise stress.

10. Use the Jumpmetrics evaluation (page 24) before, during, and after a training phase to track your progress.

Basis of the Jumpmetrics Training Approach

The name *Jumpmetrics* indicates that there will be jumping involved in the plan. This section will provide you with insight on how the variables of exercise are managed within the plan to create a safe and productive training program.

Variables That Affect the Intensity of Exercise

• **Type of exercise.** Some plyometric exercises are low in intensity while others are more stressful and therefore categorized as high intensity. The Jumpmetrics plan provides a variety of exercises that cover the entire spectrum of training intensity. The athlete uses low-intensity exercises in the early phases of the plan and then progresses to greater exercise intensities over time.

• **Number of exercises performed during a workout.** Jumpmetrics uses a very low number of direct takeoff and landing exercises per training day. The emphasis of the program is to ensure a high quality of movement. The important thing to learn from the exercise experience is the proper postural alignment of the joints during performance. Exercises in the beginning of the program concentrate on sagittal plane takeoffs and landings. As the athlete progresses, movements begin to graduate toward the frontal plane and then finally to transverse plane activities (figure 4.2). A large number

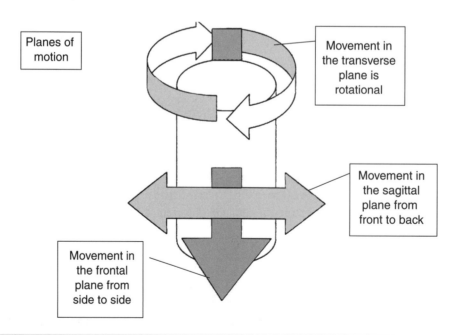

Figure 4.2 Planes of motion involved in Jumpmetrics training.

of movements is unnecessary because the objective in this area of training is to reinforce neural patterns and enhance neural drive, not to create an environment of muscular exhaustion.

- **Increases in exercise repetitions and sets.** Exercise sets and repetitions are increased over the course of the program, but for the same reasons previously described, they are never increased as a means of creating exhaustion. Increases are used to ensure that the athlete continues to perform an adequate amount of work to maintain the skill.

- **Type of takeoff and landing surfaces (hard or soft).** Takeoff and landing surfaces should always be considered. A softer landing surface will reduce physical stress on the body. Eventually, however, athletes must train on the surface that they play on to ensure that the training is realistic.

- **Height of takeoffs and landings.** In the beginning, takeoffs and landings should be low to the ground for any athlete. The inexperienced athlete will need to keep jump heights lower for a longer period than the more experienced athlete. Low jump height exercises such as jumping rope or skipping are great for introducing plyometric activity to the athlete.

- **Rest between sets of an exercise.** More intense plyometric work requires more rest between sets of exercises. The intensity of plyometric work can be determined by considering the following guidelines:

1. Plyometric exercises performed on two legs are less intense than exercises performed on one leg.

2. In-place movements are less intense than movements that cover distance.

3. Movements performed low to the ground are less intense than movements performed higher off the ground.

4. Movements performed primarily with a single joint (e.g., ankle bounce) are less intense than movements performed with multiple joints (e.g., jumps).

5. Upper body plyometrics are more intense than lower body plyometrics.

These guidelines can help the athlete understand how the intensity of exercise is managed within the Jumpmetrics plan, and how even small changes in the same exercise can lead to added physical improvements.

Schools of Thought on Plyometric Intensity

The Jumpmetrics plan is designed to follow the suggestion of the National Strength and Conditioning Association (NSCA) that exercises should be performed on a stress continuum divided into levels of intensity. Low-intensity exercises are performed while standing in place on two feet; high-intensity exercises are performed on one foot while moving.

Some research suggests that the best measurement of plyometric intensity is the number of jumps or how many times the feet hit the ground during a workout session. Many athletes use training programs that include more foot contacts than the Jumpmetrics plan provides. The goal of the plan is to provide an adequate number of foot contacts to ensure that the athlete benefits, while minimizing the risk of overfatigue. If the athlete becomes too fatigued as a result of the training, the form of the movement will suffer. This will reinforce bad movement skills rather than creating good ones. More work is not always better; in plyometric type training, it is essential that the quality of the work outweighs the quantity. Most important, this management of footfalls will help to reduce the potential for injury during training.

Advancing through the plan, the athlete will graduate to more complex skills. In the beginning, the focus of the training is to ensure that the athlete is working within acceptable ranges of postural alignment. Basic movements are used that allow the athletes to see and feel their landings and takeoffs. As the athlete progresses, movements become transitional (e.g., the athlete is expected to move from an agility or foot speed movement directly into a jumping movement). These more complex movement skills are similar to sports skills. In sports, athletes must make smooth transitions from one type of activity to another. It is usually during this transitional period that unprepared athletes have breakdowns in balance and strength—and become injured.

An athlete at the advanced level of the Jumpmetrics plan will rarely jump and land in a straight line and will seldom start a jump or land on both feet. This athlete will often twist his body in order to turn in midair from a one-leg takeoff, and subsequently land while partially turning. The complexity of these landings and takeoffs is increased to prepare athletes for contact with other players or to increase their ability to control a racket, stick, or ball. Not every issue can be addressed during an athlete's training—only the sport itself can provide the final level of preparation. The Jumpmetrics plan provides a systematic increase in intensity over time to address sports play.

Taking off from the ground and landing are important to all sports, but not every athlete performs these skills with efficient and safe form. Jumpmetrics training should first provide a sense of body awareness that helps you realize when you are in an unsafe position. Over time the training will help you progress to higher levels of sensitivity that will allow you to make smooth transitions from one sports movement to another with the utmost safety. Improving your movement technique and body awareness will also increase your ability to move faster and with more power. Proper postural alignment ensures that energy is efficiently transferred from the ground through the body, resulting in explosive muscular power.

The Power Is On

Power is an ability made more effective by improving strength, fluidity of movement, and coordination (i.e., balance and agility). Strength and coordination of the muscles create speed, and this in turn results in power. Power is defined as the amount of distance covered over time. To cover more distance quickly, you have to move faster, and this means you are more powerful. Many people assume that larger athletes can produce more power. However, it is often the smaller athletes who have a better command over their own body weight. Because of this muscle control, the smaller athlete can create greater limb speed and increased levels of velocity, resulting in higher power outputs.

Power is therefore produced less from the amount of muscle you have, and more from how well you control those muscles. Having more muscle may help, but the amount or weight of the muscle cannot supercede the ability of the weakest muscle to perform the movement. For example, when performing an activity such as running, if your thighs are heavily muscular, this makes you very strong at the knee. But if your hip is unable to lift your thigh, you begin to lose power. If you play a sport where raising the leg up high is important, then heavily muscled thighs may actually slow you down. For this reason, in the Jumpmetrics plan, power is considered to be more about developing the nervous system than increasing muscle mass. The focus is on increasing the ability of the nerve to deliver clearer messages to the muscle faster. Therefore, activities involving balance and rapid changes of direction make up the base of training. Having both muscle and neural development is good; however, it's important to realize which one is more important for your sport and which type of training should make up the bulk of your workouts.

Terms

The following terms are often used to describe the jump or plyometric exercises and the intensity or direction of the plyometric techniques. Before you begin training, you should understand these terms to help you on your way.

Bound: Bounds are hops performed by leaving the ground off one leg and landing some distance away on the opposite leg. Bounds can be performed laterally (to the side) or forward or backward.

Bounce: A bounce is a less intense version of a jump, hop, or bound. Usually, bounces are quick, low-intensity, rebounding movements used to initiate a more intense action. Bounces are also used to provide a "springiness" to an action or movement.

Hop: You perform a hop off one foot, and depending on the intensity of the exercise, you can land on the same foot or on two feet. Also depending on the exercise intensity, a hop can be performed vertically and in place for height or horizontally for distance.

Jump: You perform a jump off two feet, and you usually land on two feet. Depending on the exercise intensity and objectives, a jump can be performed vertically and in place for height or horizontally for distance.

Leap: A leap is an action where, after leaving the ground, you change your leg position in midair by swinging, kicking, or lifting.

Exercises

The following exercises are used in each of the various levels of the Jumpmetrics plan. These exercises are described in detail; however, if you are unsure of how the exercise is performed, you should seek the advice of a certified strength and conditioning coach or personal trainer. The purpose of the following exercises is to properly condition your neuromuscular system to deliver clearly directed information from your nerves to the working muscles. This information will create greater energy transfer, allowing you to move more smoothly and powerfully.

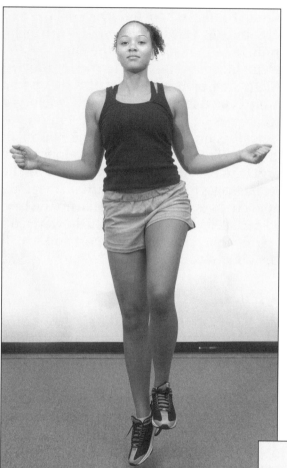

Jump Rope (Two Feet or One Foot)

Jump rope in the traditional fashion. Jump and land on two feet, or as a variation, jump and land on one foot.

Broad Jump

This is a two-legged long jump. Jump off and land on two feet every jump. Swing your arms and rock on your heels forward and back to create momentum to help you jump farther. Attempt to acquire some vertical height on your jumps to improve your horizontal distance. When you land, strike the floor with your heels first and then roll toward your toes and allow your knees to bend. These landing techniques will reduce the amount of impact on the body.

Cycle Jumps

Begin with one foot in front and the other foot behind. Both knees should be slightly bent. Jump up and in midair switch the position of the legs, landing with the opposite foot in front. When you land, strike the floor with the balls of the feet, and then allow your heels to hit and allow your knees to bend. These landing techniques will reduce the amount of impact on the body. Landing on a semisoft mat can also reduce the stress of landing. The jump can be very small in the beginning to help you become accustomed to switching the legs (almost like a lunge exercise with a jump after). As you progress, you should jump for height and allow the feet to kick up and strike the buttocks while in the air. This will promote body control and quickness.

One-Leg Long Jump

Perform a series of long jumps while standing on one leg. Jump off the same leg each time and always land on both feet. Jump five times and measure the distance achieved. See how much distance you can cover in five jumps. Try to better your distance on each leg every set. Swing your arms and free leg forward and back, and then use the momentum of a forward swing to help you jump farther. Attempt to acquire some vertical height on your jumps to improve your horizontal distance.

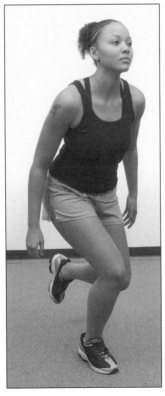

Power Skips

Begin by raising the arms and one knee upward quickly. At the same time, hop vertically up and off the floor using the support leg. Land on the same leg you took off on. When you land, quickly pull the arms up again and raise the knee of the opposite leg (the one that was the support leg). This time hop vertically upward off the new support leg. Repeat the action for a given distance or a given number of times. The emphasis should be on moving vertically as high as you can. This means that while moving (skipping) a given horizontal distance, you are trying to perform as many vertical leaps as possible.

Tuck Jump

Jump up and tuck the legs near the chest while suspended in air. To emphasize the tuck, loosely hug the knees. This hug must be performed quickly in order to not impede the landing. When you land on this and all other plyometric exercises, allow the knees to bend a little to absorb the impact.

Vertical Jumps (With Step or No Step)

This is a standard vertical jump. The exercise can be performed with both feet side by side and stationary or with the nondominant leg in front and the dominant leg stepping forward to create momentum for the jump. Rapid rebound jumping is not beneficial here. It is critical to make each jump count. The key to creating a strong jump is in how quickly you can change directions when moving into the down and then back into the up position. Also, you must remain relaxed; using too much muscle creates tension and the jump height is reduced.

Half-Spin Jump

Jump up, and while in the air, spin the body around and land facing the opposite direction. This is a great developer of body control and awareness. This also profoundly affects your balance. You can spin to your right or to your left.

One-Leg Vertical Takeoff

Run a few steps and then jump off one leg. Set a target, and attempt to touch it (use a vertical jump tester for accurate achievement measures). Use the hand opposite the starting (takeoff) leg to touch the target. This ensures proper weight distribution and balance during the exercise.

Ankle Bounce (One Foot)

Standing in place, use only the ankles to create an upward bouncing movement. As soon as you touch the ground, rapidly rebound into another bounce. A pad can be placed on the floor to land on. Padded surfaces will prevent overstressing the body and make plyometric training less stressful for the beginner.

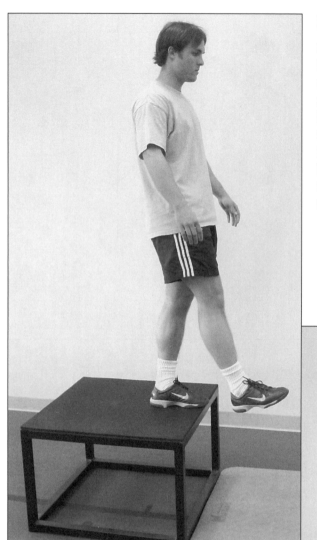

Depth Jumps

Stand on a box or other stable object (start with a low height and move up in height gradually). Step off the edge and land on both feet with your knees bent and your arms straight out in front. A cushioned mat can reduce the initial impact stress of the exercise. Later, the mat can be taken away to add more intensity. This exercise is stressful and should be used sparingly. It is important that you bend your knees when landing to absorb the impact and to allow the muscle to absorb the load. This loading on the muscle will benefit its neural and reactive abilities.

Full-Spin Jump

Jump up and spin the body completely around while in the air. Land facing the same direction as when you started. You can spin to your right or to your left.

Lateral Bounce

Stand with your legs about shoulder-width apart, with one foot on each side of a line. Stay over the line and bounce quickly from one foot to the other (similar to the ankle bounce movement). Perform this movement in place (see photo at right). Each foot should leave and return to the floor in the same place.

Ice-Skaters

This is an expanded version of the lateral bounce. The distance the body travels is greater in this exercise—you must land farther out on each side of the line. While staying low to the ground, bound laterally, leaving the ground with the left foot and landing on the right foot. Then move back to the left, pushing off the right foot. The leg coming behind the leg on the floor helps to swing the body to the side and makes it easier to jump.

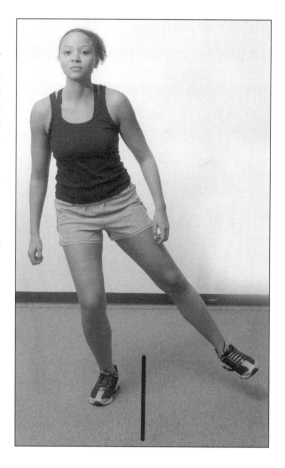

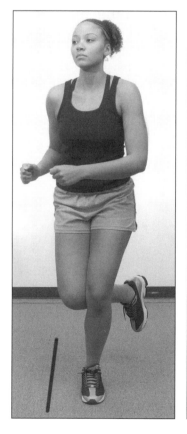

Lateral Hops

Hop on one foot from side to side. This action can be done over a line or over an object of a specified height. As you become more advanced, the distance that you hop laterally can be extended.

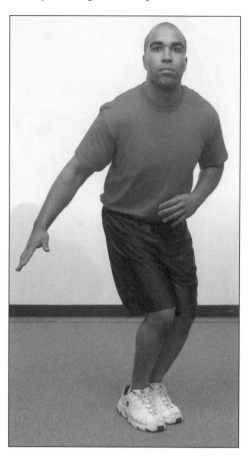

Mogul Hops (Small)

Begin with the body straight and the hips turned slightly to the left. The knees should be bent and the feet close together (similar to a skiing position—see photo left). Jump into the air and twist the hips to the left. Land in the same bent knee position. Continue jumping, alternately twisting the hips to the left and right. This exercise is implemented to help you feel more secure when landing in an alternative position (other than a straight torso and hip posture).

Sock Twist

Perform this exercise in stocking feet, on a semislick surface (e.g., hardwood floor, tile). You will be moving sideways. Begin the movement by twisting the hips and pointing the heels in the direction you intend to go. Twist the hips again to point the toes in the direction you intend to go. Rapidly switch heel and toes, causing the body to do "the twist" down the floor. Keep the knees bent. This exercise will effectively work the internal and external rotators of the hips and provide a little fun in the training session. The arms should be bent at the elbows and held up with the upper arms parallel to the floor.

Zigzag Jump

Moving forward, zigzag by jumping on two feet from side to side (see figure at right). This action can be done over a line or over an object of a specified height (e.g., a line of hurdles or a rope suspended over the ground). You are moving forward as you jump from side to side. As you become more advanced, the distance that you jump from side to side can be extended.

Two-Foot Twist Hop

Jump forward on both feet. Twist your hips but attempt to keep your upper torso facing in the direction you are moving. This action can be done over a line or over an object such as a four-inch hurdle or string to increase the difficulty. This exercise is a much more controlled activity than jumping for a rebound and being forced to land on one foot in a twisting position as a result of contact.

One-Foot Twist Hop

Jump forward on one foot. Twist your hips but attempt to keep your upper torso facing in the direction you are moving. This action can be done over a line or an object.

One-Foot Hop With Rotations

Move forward on one foot while hopping in 45-degree incremented rotations (eight hops to make a full turn) until you have completed a 360-degree circle. Rotate eight hops toward your left shoulder, and then eight hops toward your right shoulder.

One-Leg Tuck Jump

Jump high (straight up) off one foot by first flexing rapidly at the knee, hip, and ankle. Thrust your arms upward to help lift your body from the ground. While in the air, attempt to quickly pull your knees to your chest. Land softly on one foot by allowing the knee, ankle, and hip to flex on contact with the floor to absorb some of your landing force.

Two-Legged Sideways Broad Jump

Jump off two feet laterally. Use the arms to provide lift by flexing them upward. Land softly on impact by hitting the ground with a toe-heel contact, and allow the knees to bend. Repeat the jumps for an assigned distance before returning in the opposite direction. As you become more advanced, the distance that you jump to the side can be extended.

5

Jumpmetrics Training to Optimize Balance and Agility

Balance is the key to athletic success. An athlete is only as successful as the base on which she stands. However, balance is the most forgotten and neglected aspect of most athletes' training plans. Introducing balance training into your plan is the best way to optimize your potential power. Jumpmetrics puts balance work in the forefront of the training protocol.

Like any other physical ability, your balance can be developed and improved. Some balance drills in the Jumpmetrics plan are performed in place, and others are performed while moving. Of course, the more an athlete is forced to move during balance training, the more difficult and complex the movement becomes.

Most of the balance drills in the plan are performed on one foot. One-foot training makes maintaining your balance more challenging, and if you can improve your balance on one foot, you can more easily balance yourself on two feet. If you feel comfortable and you have no injuries, the in-place balance activities should be performed without shoes. Shoes provide support to the ankle and foot, which is good when performing in a sport; however, because shoes provide such good support, the muscles that control movement of the ankles and feet are often required to work less to help you balance. This can make those muscles weak and less effective. Conditions may not allow working without shoes, but performing the movements without shoes will force the stabilizing muscles of the ankle to work harder to maintain your balance, thus increasing their strength. The countermovements used to maintain your balance are also transferred into the knees, hips, and lower back. Balance training therefore benefits the entire lower body.

In the beginning of training, your lack of familiarity with the movements and postures will provide adequate stimulus to enhance your balance. As you progress, additional destabilizers can be employed to ensure continued advancements.

© Charles Small/SportsChrome

Athletes can benefit from using their game objects while training with Jumpmetrics.

Perturbation training is an excellent method of challenging your ability to maintain balance. A *perturbation* is a disturbance of motion, such as an applied external force, used to destabilize the athlete. This force can be applied through the expected or unexpected contact with another person or object. While balancing, the application of small pushes and nudges, or catching and throwing an object, can mimic contact events common to sports. Perturbation training is an essential progression when training athletes. Sports create unpredictable environments. Player-to-player contact, catching, throwing, and changing directions while holding or managing a ball or sports implement make balancing all the more difficult.

Athletes who manage some type of object (e.g., ball, stick, or racket) during play should use that object during advanced training. In the beginning, when you are learning to perform the drills proficiently, it makes little sense to use the object during exercise. First build your skill level in the drill, and then begin to incorporate the ball, stick, or other sport implement.

The Jumpmetrics plan takes into account that when an athlete plays, the body sometimes turns when it lands. This essentially creates a blind landing for the athlete. Turning the head causes inner ear disturbance, making the act of balancing more difficult. Some of the balance exercises are therefore performed with the eyes closed or while turning the head. Without sight, you are forced to depend more on the feedback from the muscles and joints.

Exercises

Balance is the most integral part of the Jumpmetrics program. Without proper balance, the athlete is continuously wasting energy. Sports are never played on two feet. The athlete is continuously moving from one foot to the other. Without balance, speed and power are repeatedly lost. Good balance also plays a critical role in the safety and surefootedness of the athlete. If the knee, hip, and ankle are forced out of alignment at a critical moment during a sports movement, injury could occur. Having proper balance can protect the athlete by giving him better body awareness and strength in the deeper muscles (synergist muscles) that stabilize, neutralize, or work to assist the action of other movements. *Synergists* are muscles that perform work away from the primary movement, but they act to pull the joint or other tissues in a way that facilitates the primary muscle action.

Proper center of gravity (COG) is essential to performance. Center of gravity is the perfect point in space where the height and width of your posture or stance provide the most stability. The center of gravity for the board on a seesaw is somewhere in the middle of the board. When you are in an upright position, a higher COG can produce faster times and reactions, but it can also make it more difficult to control your balance (which can slow you back down). Squatting lower into an athletic stance or posture can make you more balanced, but it can cause you to become slower because this posture keeps your feet more firmly pressed into the ground. Understanding how to manage your COG can make all the difference in how you perform. A good rule for training is to perform lower-stance work for strength and higher-stance work for balance—but play somewhere in between a high and low stance (in the middle) to perform with both speed and strength.

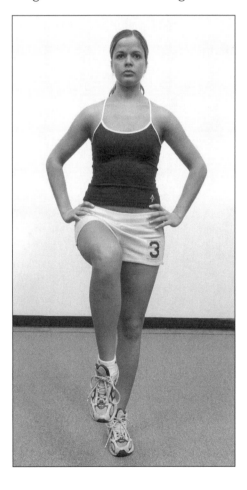

In-Place Exercises

In-place exercises are performed while standing in one location. These exercises are the most simple of the balance exercises.

One-Foot Balance

Simply stand on one foot. Keep the knee of the free leg up with the upper thigh parallel to the floor (see figure at right). This will raise your center of gravity, making the exercise more difficult. Also place the hands on the hips to narrow the center of gravity. Raising and narrowing your center of gravity make the exercise more challenging.

One-Foot Balance With Head Turn

Perform the one-foot balance exercise, but turn your head to the left and right. Look for targets over your left and right shoulders. This will cause your visual field to shift, making balancing more difficult, and causing you to rely more on your proprioceptive abilities (how the movement feels) rather than sight to balance you.

One-Foot Balance With Eyes Closed

Perform the one-foot balance exercise, but close your eyes. This will make you depend on what you feel your body doing to produce balance (rather than what you see to stabilize it).

One-Foot Balance on Balance Disc

Perform the one-foot balance exercise, but stand on a balance disc inflatable pad to make the surface more unpredictable. Keep the knee of the free leg up with the upper thigh parallel to the floor. This will raise your center of gravity, making the exercise more difficult. Also place the hands on the hips to narrow the center of gravity.

Half Squat on One Foot

Stand on one foot and place the free leg in one of three positions:

1. Behind you on a bench, or for added difficulty, on a large exercise ball
2. Behind you with the foot of the free leg pressed tightly into the back of the supporting leg's ankle
3. Fully extended in front of you (this is the most difficult position)

With the free leg placed in one of the three positions, bend the knee, hip, and ankle of the support leg to lower the buttocks toward the floor. The top of the thigh of the support leg should be almost parallel to the floor, and the knee should be behind the toes and in line with the second toe of the support foot. Both arms can be fully extended in front of the body to counterbalance the posterior (to the rear) shift of the body weight.

One-Quarter Squat on One Foot

This exercise is the same as the half squat exercise, except the support leg bends less at the knee, and the upper thigh does not have to be parallel to the floor.

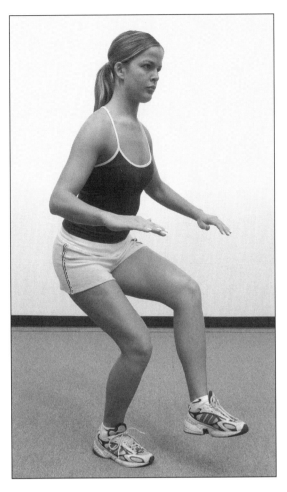

One-Foot Fire Brigade

This is a passing drill where two or more athletes stand on one foot in a straight line and pass a medicine ball to one another by twisting at the hips and turning on the support leg. At first, the athletes can just hand the ball to one another. They can then progress to throwing the ball along the line in a more advanced form of the exercise.

One-Foot Balance With Medicine Ball Toss

Balance on one foot, keeping the thigh of the free leg parallel to the floor. Toss the medicine ball back and forth with a partner (coach or another athlete).

One-Leg Quarter Squat With Medicine Ball Toss

Perform a one-leg quarter squat, and while holding the posture, toss a medicine ball back and forth with a partner. This is similar to perturbation training in that you will not be sure of the direction or the force of the incoming ball until it reaches you. The corresponding "jolt" will cause you to correct your balance and strengthen the hips, knees, and ankles.

Half Squat (Knee Wiper)

Perform a half squat on one leg. Make sure to sit back and let the hip take the brunt of the body's weight. Counterbalance your tendency to fall backward in this posture by fully extending the arms in front of you. Having the arms out in front is better because the counterbalance weight of your arms allows you to move your buttocks back farther, thus helping you keep your knee behind your toes. Don't extend the knee past the toes; keep it in line with the second toe. If you are unable to do this, do not continue with the knee wiper—just hold the squat to build your strength in the exercise. If you have postural control, allow the knee to drift in slightly toward the midline of the body and then pull the knee back out again. The knee wiper is designed to strengthen the hip and provide kinesthetic awareness of where the knee is positioned during the movement.

Lateral Reach

Perform a one-leg squat while extending the free leg out to the side to touch the ground with the toe pointed. Push the hip and buttock of the support leg back as far as possible. The arms can be held out in front to improve the balance required for the movement.

Four Point Touch

Stand on one foot and bend the supporting knee, making sure the knee doesn't extend past the toes and the knee stays in line with the second toe of the foot. The other knee is up, with the thigh parallel to the ground. Sit back to ensure that the gluteals perform at their best to stabilize the upper leg. After you bend the knee, reach down and touch the floor in front of you, then stand back up. Look to the left and then bend the knee and use the left hand to touch the floor to your left. Stand back up, look to your right, and bend to touch the floor with your right hand. Return to the standing posture, and then look at the heel of your foot. Bend the knee again and, using either hand, reach back to touch the floor as far back as possible between your feet. Repeat this series with the other leg supporting.

Multidirectional Kick

While firmly balanced on one leg, perform a front (*a*), side (*b*), and back (*c*) kick one after the other with the free leg. Repeat the kicks for the assigned duration, and never set the kicking leg down for support during that time. Repeat with the other leg.

Multidirectional Kick on Balance Disc

Perform the multidirectional kick exercise, but stand on a balance disc to perform the kicks.

Turning Exercises

Turning requires a change in foot position that makes balancing more challenging. When you turn, you should attempt to stand on the ball of your foot and then, using a subtle hip and arm motion, turn your body to face another direction. Turning on the ball of your foot reduces surface contact, making balancing even more difficult. After turning, set back down on your full foot to reestablish balance.

Quarter Turn

Stand on one foot with the free leg up so the upper thigh is parallel to the ground. Put your hands on your hips. Rise up on the toes of the support leg and twist the hips to make a quarter turn in the direction of the free leg. Set down on the heel to rebalance yourself. After the assigned number of turns in the direction of the free leg, perform the turns in the opposite direction.

Half Turn (180 Degrees)

Stand on one foot with the free leg up so the upper thigh is parallel to the ground. Put your hands on your hips. Rise up on the toes of the support leg and twist the hips to make a 180-degree turn in the direction of the free leg (so you are facing the opposite direction). Set down on the heel to rebalance yourself. After the assigned number of turns in the direction of the free leg, perform the turns in the opposite direction.

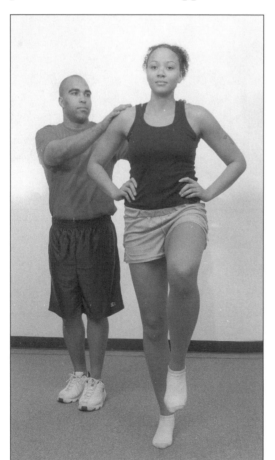

Quarter Turn With Perturbations

Perform the quarter-turn exercise, but have a partner stand behind you and lightly push or pull your upper shoulders. These surprise changes of force will help strengthen your hips, knees, and ankles and help you adapt to similar surprise stressors that sports actions will place on you. Injuries can occur when you are bumped during play and you aren't prepared to counter the force placed on you. (Kicks provide challenges to balance by forcing you to lean opposite of the direction of the kick to maintain balance.)

Quarter-Turn Back Kick

Stand on one foot with the free leg up so the upper thigh is parallel to the ground *(a)*. Put your hands on your hips. Rise up on the toes of the support leg and twist the hips to make a quarter turn in the direction of the free leg *(b)*. Set down on the heel to rebalance yourself. Look over your shoulder on the free leg side and extend the free leg straight back behind you with the foot dorsiflexed (toe toward the shin). Your hands can come off your hips as you kick *(c)*. Return the kicking leg to the front of the body with the knee up, and prepare for the next quarter turn. Continue turning in the same direction as the original turn. Kicks provide challenges to balance by forcing you to lean in the opposite direction of the kick to maintain balance.

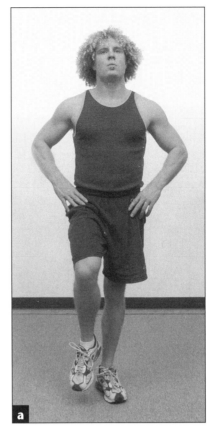

Quarter-Turn Back Kick With Ground Touch

Perform the quarter-turn back kick exercise. After every kick, continue to hold the leg fully extended, turn your head back to the front, look down, and then touch the floor with the hand opposite of the extended leg. (Do the drill without shoes to challenge your balance at a higher level.)

Hopping Exercises

Balance exercises that require you to move into them are the next step (level of difficulty) in balance training. The same detail to body position and posture that was demonstrated in the previous exercises should apply here as well.

Hop Stick Landing

Hop forward and land on one foot. When you land, attempt to be as quiet as possible. This soft landing is accomplished by first swinging the arms upward from the hips when you jump. The added lift that the upper body provides will give you time to steady your landing. When you land, allow the knee to bend on impact to absorb the weight of the body. Land on the ball of the foot and then transfer that energy by allowing your heel to come down next. This soft landing should allow you full body control, and you should not have to double hop or slide the foot from side to side to maintain balance. You should avoid unbalanced landings during this drill. Hop forward for the assigned distance or number of repetitions.

Hop Stick Landing With Side Kick

Perform the hop stick landing exercise, but after each landing, pull the knee of the free leg high to the chest, and then slowly kick the leg out to the side, keeping the foot flexed. Allow the hips to twist slightly upward on the free leg side to facilitate the kick.

a

Hop Stick Landing With Back Kick

Perform the hop stick landing exercise, but after each landing, hop in place, spin, and land again on the same foot so that you face the opposite direction (you then perform a back kick before spinning back to face the original direction). Stand on one foot throughout the exercise and try to keep the free knee held high (upper thigh parallel to the floor) (*a*). Hop forward onto one foot (the same foot you are standing on). Next, jump in place and turn 180 degrees to face the opposite direction (*b*). Looking over your shoulder on the free leg side, slowly kick back and fully extend your free leg. After the kick, pull the kicking leg back and remain standing on one foot (*c*). Again, jump in place and make another 180-degree turn to face the original jumping direction. Repeat the entire series on the same leg for the assigned distance or number of hops, and then perform the exercise on the opposite leg.

b

c

Ball Exercises

Performing exercise on a movable object requires a great level of body awareness. Using a balance ball can provide the ultimate challenge.

Two-Knee Balance on Ball

Attempt to balance on a large balance ball with the knees, shins, and feet in contact with the ball. The body should be held in an upright position with the hands out to the side for added body control. Use the hips in a "hula hoop" style to control the motion of the ball. When trying to balance on the ball, it may be necessary to first place the hands on the floor and gradually work toward lifting one hand from the floor at a time. This will help teach you how to adjust your hips to the subtle changes in the ball's position. Eventually, you will place your hands on the ball instead of the floor, and from there you will balance enough to assume the upright posture. Once you are able to balance, moving the hips from side to side will add to the challenge of the exercise. You can also try catching a ball, shooting a free throw, swinging a golf club or tennis racket, or performing a "Flexed T" baseball pitching position.

One-Knee Balance on Ball

This is an advanced version of the two-knee balance on ball exercise. In this version, you support yourself on one knee instead of two. This requires much more hip strength and stability and should not be attempted until the double knee version is fully mastered.

6

Dynamic Power Warm-Ups

Dynamic flexibility exercises are assigned as a warm-up routine prior to the beginning of each Jumpmetrics workout session. The exercises require the athlete to move through the sagittal, frontal, and transverse planes of human motion, while at the same time coordinating muscle tension and relaxation patterns.

The warm-up is always a critical part of exercise, not only for proper cardio-vascular health, but also for heightened skeletal muscle performance. Warm muscle tissues are less viscous, meaning they are less sticky and stiff. This tissue mobility makes the muscle more elastic. An elastic muscle has more spring or snap, generating force more rapidly. This, of course, can result in greater speed and power.

Playing a sport requires a full range of motion. An athlete's body shape, size, and level of flexibility will determine his range of motion. Athletic performance requires rapid limb movements, and these rapid movements can result in injury if the muscles involved are too resistant. An athlete's level of flexibility can be improved, but improvement requires a multidirectional approach. To optimize your performance, the Jumpmetrics plan uses both dynamic and static flexibility techniques at specific times in the training plan.

The body's muscular system is interconnected. Muscle tension in one area of the body can lead to increased tension in other areas. If the athlete is unable to reduce this tension because of poor training and preparation, his range of motion can be negatively affected.

Athletic flexibility requires more than just having long muscles. Athletes are seldom engaged in static stretching (yogalike) activities, where the movements are slow and methodically held. When an athlete moves, there must be cooperation between muscle groups. When one muscle group contracts to initiate a movement, the muscles that oppose that contraction must relax to facilitate the movement. Therefore, an athlete needs to engage in dynamic or moving flexibility exercises that help to improve this contract–relax relationship between the muscle groups.

Sitting on the floor and stretching the hamstrings is good, but during a weight-bearing athletic activity, your body weight can affect other muscles that indirectly place tension on the hamstrings. For example, hip flexors forced to support your body weight can keep the hips from fully rotating backward, in turn pulling the body forward and minimizing hamstring range of motion. When considering corrective flexibility exercises, it's important to consider how the muscles behave in relation to other muscles during athletic movement. If these relationships are not managed, injury can occur.

Each of the Jumpmetrics dynamic warm-up exercises involve movements that are part of most sports. The performance of these exercises reinforces neuromuscular patterns and reduces movement inhibitions. This means that the exercises are actually controlled athletic movements, and they mimic the same action (neuromuscular patterns) as sports movements. These similar movement patterns can assist in synchronizing the flexibility and contraction relationships between the muscle groups. Improving these relationships provides less inhibition; in other words, it makes the movements smoother. Unlike common sports movements that repeat the same movement patterns over and over again, these dynamic flexibility exercises provide controlled movements through a wider variety of ranges, which can strengthen and stretch the muscles and reduce the chances of injury.

© David's Photography

Dynamic flexibility exercises involve movements used in most sports.

Performing the Dynamic Exercises

Performing the Jumpmetrics dynamic warm-up exercises correctly requires balance and good posture. It is important to get every part of the body working together to perform the dynamic movements properly. Some basic rules need to be followed in order to make these exercises most effective.

First, you must stay tall while performing all of the dynamic exercises to avoid obstructing normal hip motion. Second, always use the arms along with the legs during each movement. If you move forward in the sagittal plane (e.g., running), the arms should move in the same plane. If you move laterally (frontal plane), the hands and arms should move laterally as well. If the legs and feet move in a circular pattern (transverse plane), such as the carioca movement, the arms should move in that same circle.

Coordinating the arms with the legs helps to accelerate and decelerate the body—this keeps the footfalls light and helps you to quickly make transitions from one foot to the next. Having the foot make less contact with the ground will require less time to move it from the ground.

Finally, unless instructed otherwise, you should attempt to be quiet during the movements. Being quiet requires muscle control that will train the muscles to be stronger and promote better body control. Some movements require a strong footfall to increase drive and force into the ground for speed. These movements cannot be quiet, and the foot should be applied to the ground with a sharp striking action. It is important for an athlete to be able to apply both types of footfalls on command. Athletes that cannot separate these two physical requirements must be made more aware of the proprioceptive (how the movement feels) difference.

In the workouts presented in chapters 8 through 10, the warm-up section will indicate that you should perform one of three dynamic lists. To identify the warm-up exercises included in each of these lists, refer to table 6.1. The description of how to perform each exercise in the lists is also provided in this chapter.

TABLE 6.1

Dynamic Warm-Up Exercise Lists

1	2	3
Form run	Form run	Backward run
Backward run	Backward run	Tapioca (rapid-fire carioca)
Carioca	Slo-mo outside-in	Knee raise to elbows
Inside hip flip	Slo-mo outside-out	Goose step
Outside hip flip	Carioca skip with or without floor pop	Slow low step slide
Butt kick	Ankling	High fast step slide
Skip forward or backward	A-skip	Knee grab

Duration and Intensity of the Exercises

The intensity of each dynamic warm-up exercise in the lists is determined by how well you perform the movement. In the beginning, certain inflexibilities and weaknesses will make the exercises difficult for you. As you become stronger and more flexible, you should focus even more closely on the three rules just described concerning posture, arm actions, and weight of your footfalls. Focusing on these areas can keep the exercise difficulty high until you master all three actions at once while performing. As you become better at the movements, you will find that the intensity lessens.

Each exercise should be performed for a given distance. We suggest a distance of 15 to 20 yards. This means you will always be moving forward when you perform each movement. You could make the distance longer, but it is more important to perform these exercises properly before moving to greater distances. The goal with these exercises is perfect performance. If fatigue becomes too great, you will reestablish bad movement habits that can hurt your performance.

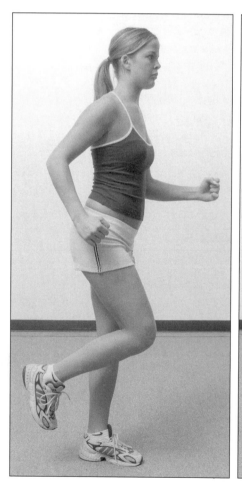

Form Run

Run at a low speed. Hold the arms at 90-degree angles as a frame to focus the upper torso's direction in the sagittal plane (in a straight path). Stride out and concentrate on lifting the knees. The foot should be held in dorsiflexion (toe toward shin) while the knee is up. The foot should strike the ground on the ball of the foot and roll forward forcing you off the ground. As the foot leaves the ground, raise the front knee while pulling the back foot up in a snapping motion toward the buttocks.

Backward Run

Run backward at a low speed in a low crouching position, keeping the head forward and well over the feet. Bend the arms at 90-degree angles to frame the upper torso (in this exercise, you must run away from the frame rather than into it as in the form run). The foot must strike on the toe and roll back to just behind the ball of the foot before leaving the ground.

Carioca

This exercise is traditionally referred to as the *grapevine*. Start with the feet shoulder-width apart and move laterally by crossing one leg in front of the body. If traveling to the right, you'll cross your left leg in front. This becomes the down-track leg. The right leg, or the up-track leg, steps out so the feet are again shoulder-width apart. The down-track leg then moves again, this time stepping behind the up-track leg. This pattern is repeated continuously. The foot can be forced into the ground on each crossover step and should be held in a toe up position on ground strike. Because the legs are tracing a circular pattern, the arms should be held at chest level and should form a hugging arc to mimic the same circular pattern.

Inside Hip Flip

Lift one knee and flip your free leg up and across the centerline of your body as if to kick your opposite hand with the inside of your shoe. Alternate legs while walking forward. Remain loose in the kicking leg throughout the movement. This exercise will stretch the kicking leg at the hip. In addition, the rotation of the support leg will make it stronger. While doing this exercise, hold the arms in a relaxed position at your side.

Outside Hip Flip

Perform a rotational kick with the knees pressed together and the lifted knee pointing downward to the floor. Alternate legs while walking forward. The foot moves in a curved path to the side and back as if to kick yourself on the outside buttock. This exercise will stretch the kicking leg at the hip and groin. In addition, the rotation of the support leg will make it stronger, both externally and internally. Hold the arms in a relaxed position at your side.

Butt Kick

Move forward while performing butt kicks. Alternate legs and bring the heel behind the body and up toward the buttocks. The foot should be held in a dorsiflexed (toe up toward the shin) position during the entire movement. This exercise promotes quadriceps flexibility. The hands should be held palms outward away from the body at the buttocks.

Knee Grab

Walk forward, remaining very upright, and lift and pull the knees in to the chest, alternating legs each step. Keep the toe up and toward the shin (dorsiflexed).

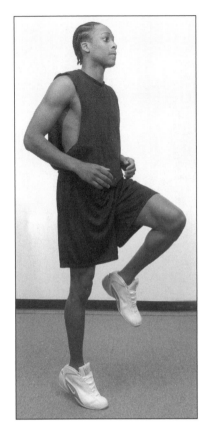

Skip Forward or Backward

Skipping is a tempo or rhythm movement performed by stepping with one foot and then making a small one- to two-inch hop onto that same foot. This is a very simple movement for some athletes, but for other athletes the motor program was never introduced or was lost through the years. This foot pattern can be repeated either forward or backward. Keeping the foot in dorsiflexion and making the foot strikes snap to the floor benefit the sprint form. The arm action in this drill should be opposite arm to opposite knee.

Slo-Mo Outside-In

This is a strength and flexibility exercise. Moving laterally, raise the leg that is away from the direction being moved up and away from the midline of the body. Imagine a large ball in front of you—as you raise the leg, it will be coming up on one side of the imaginary ball. At the midline of the body, as the leg crosses the top of the ball, the leg should be fully extended at the knee. (The knee should be slightly flexed to begin the movement and then straighten. As the foot gets to the midway point, the knee is then flexed again after it hits the peak height of the movement.) As the leg crosses the midline, it begins to bend again to finish toward the wall in front of you. In this exercise, the support leg receives strengthening of the internal and external rotators, and the free leg is dynamically stretched and strengthened in the hip flexors and quadriceps. Move ahead laterally after each kick (by stepping with the support leg) to cover the assigned distance.

Slo-Mo Inside-Out

This is a strength and flexibility exercise. Moving laterally, raise the leg (knee flexed) that is toward the direction being moved up and across the midline of the body. Again, imagine a large ball in front of you—as you raise the leg, it will be coming up on one side of the imaginary ball. At the midline of the body, as the leg crosses the top of the ball, the leg should be fully extended at the knee. As the leg crosses the midline, it begins to bend again, finishing with the outside of the thigh toward the wall in front of you. In this exercise, the support leg receives strengthening of the internal and external rotators, and the free leg is dynamically stretched and strengthened in the hip flexors and quadriceps.

Carioca Skip With or Without Floor Pop

This exercise is a carioca with a small hop on each footfall. As one leg crosses the midline of the body, the knee should remain high and close to the body. The foot crossing the midline can be sharply planted on the ground in a dorsiflexed position to simulate the leg drive and force required in sprinting.

Ankling

This exercise is a rapid and forceful heel raise. With the legs nearly straight, move from one foot to the other, forcing your body from the ground using only the power of the ankle. Explosive opposite arm to leg motion will assist in raising the body from the ground. Like all forward motion exercises, the arms should be held at 90-degree angles at the elbow.

A-Skip

March forward with high knees. When the knee is lifted, hop with the supporting leg.

Tapioca (Rapid-Fire Carioca)

This exercise is a carioca with shorter steps. The hips must be twisted during the movement. Remember to keep the arm moving in a short circular arc across the body at chest level.

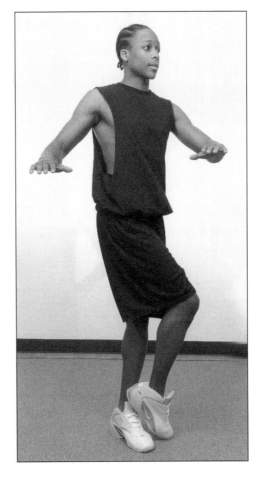

Knee Raise to Elbows

Walk forward with your hands clasped behind your head. Bring one knee up and out to the side toward the elbow on the same side. Keep the body tall. The exercise is intended to dynamically stretch the gluteal and posterior hips and to strengthen the hip flexors in the upper leg.

Goose Step

Walk forward on the soles of the feet with the arms stretched out in front of you. On each step, keep the legs straight, and kick forward attempting to touch the outstretched hand with your foot—but only bring the leg up as far as you can while it remains straight. The body should stay tall and forward (do not twist) as you move forward. You do not need to kick high. Only kick as high as the straight leg will comfortably allow. Dorsiflex the foot toward the shin. Do not bend forward to touch the feet. Just stay tall and do the best you can with your legs straight. This exercise is intended to strengthen the hip flexor and quadriceps and dynamically flex the hamstrings, lower back, and gluteals.

Slow Low Step Slide

This is a strengthening exercise for the gluteals, quadriceps, adductors, abductors, and hamstrings. Moving laterally, remain low as if under a low ceiling. The lead foot steps laterally, and the trailing leg is dragged across the ground. This dragging of the trail leg will work the inner thigh more effectively. Hold the arms in front of the body and use gentle lateral arm movements to counterbalance the weight of the body. The feet should remain wide—never allow the trail leg to come forward beside the lead leg (see photo at left). This movement is the same as a defensive step slide used when playing basketball.

High Fast Step Slide

Perform a step slide in the same fashion as the slow version, but use a higher stance and faster foot motions. This exercise promotes tempo and transfer of energy. It should help you stay light on your feet while moving sideways. Stay on the balls of the feet and move the arms laterally in rhythm with the feet. This is similar to a basketball defensive slide.

7

Jumpmetrics Workout Plan

There are countless ways to design a workout plan. Postures and exercises used to improve your strength and performance are of little value by themselves. Unless exercises are organized into progressive routines that provide increases in intensity over time, your workout plan will fall short of helping you achieve your goals.

The Jumpmetrics plan is unique because the workout intensity is progressive in two ways. The first method of workout progression is established using workout *levels*. The levels are different workout programs that are assigned to the athlete to take her through an increase in intensity over the entire span of the Jumpmetrics plan (see table 7.1). Each athlete should perform each of the levels in its entirety. If an athlete scored poorly on the evaluation from chapter 2, she must be more aware of her body position when performing an exercise or routine. If the athlete scores well on the evaluation, she would still do all the exercises performed by the athlete with the lower score, but she can proceed through the drills at a faster and more athletic rate. Each athlete should complete the entire program to ensure that all postures are learned and that the critical element of balance is promoted.

The second form of progression within each level is to assign more challenging exercises each passing week. Strength movements are made more intense through changes in work volume (increased number of repetitions and sets). The intensity level of balance and power movements can be increased by adding components to the movements such as kicks, twists, head turns, tethering, and light resistance. Emphasizing proper form or changing the body's position during a movement can ensure heightened intensity as well.

TABLE 7.1

Emphasis in Levels

Level	Intensity and complexity	Performance	Distance of jumps	Height of jumps	Change of direction	Planes of motion
1	Low	Two-leg landings and takeoffs, twists on ground	In place or with minimal distance traveled	Low to the floor	Reserved for side-to-side two-foot jumping	Frontal and sagittal
2	Medium	One-leg hops, two-leg jumps and twists	Moving in some direction, twisting in place	From low to the floor to maximal height	Predictable one- and two-leg changes	Frontal, sagittal, and transverse
3	High	One-leg hops and twists, two-leg jumps and twists	Moving in some direction, twisting in place	From low to the floor to maximal height	Predictable and unpredictable changes	Frontal, sagittal, and transverse

The Program in Plain View

The Jumpmetrics program is presented in chapters 8 through 10 in an easy-to-read grid layout. At the top of each vertical column, you will see a training emphasis or basic skill. In each of the blocks under that basic skill, a series of exercises will be presented that will maximize your ability to achieve desirable results. Each row represents a day or single session of training. Follow the grid from left to right and complete the drills in that order.

The exercises in each box of the grid are described in the previous chapters of this book. (Additional exercises for the "Overload" column, or weekly strength programs, are presented later in this chapter.) The volumes and duration for each exercise are presented within the box of the grid. Refer to the previous chapters to review the importance of each exercise and identify how to perform each exercise. Improvements made in these exercises will enhance your athletic ability and reduce your chances for injury by developing proper muscle balance.

The Jumpmetrics plan can be performed at any time of the year, but the amount of work created in the three levels is most appropriate for a workout before or after practice during the in-season parts of the training year. Once the routine has been learned, it should take no more than 20 minutes to complete.

The overload portion of the workout can be performed before or after practice. However, because this portion of the training involves more muscular challenging resistance training, it is best to perform these exercises earlier in the training day (with at least a one- to two-hour break before the start of the practice session). Other than this exception, the order of exercise is important to ensure proper warm-up and maximal results. If you are unable to perform the overload section because your team or coach already has a resistance training requirement, you might want to do the optional postpractice strength routine included in the program. This additional work is challenging when done after practice, and it can ensure that you are addressing the muscular requirements that coincide with the Jumpmetrics plan.

Before beginning this or any other written program, you must realize that it will never be as good as receiving one-on-one instruction from a qualified coach. In a book, photos can show the exercises, but the movement skills required to perform that exercise must be continuously refined. Constant cueing from a coach with a trained eye will ensure that you are in the correct posture, and the incorrect movement patterns or habits that usually waste precious time are minimized. Sometimes locating or affording good coaching is difficult. This is why we have designed this written program to be as comprehensive as possible.

Dynamic Warm-Up

Coaches are always looking for ways to properly warm up players before practice. Jumpmetrics is designed to serve as an extensive prepractice warm-up or a postpractice cool-down.

Warming up briefly before a workout is beneficial for several reasons:

1. It warms and prepares the muscle tissue for more intense activity. By gradually warming up the muscle, you ensure that your muscles are adapting to more intense exercise.

2. Warming up before exercise has been shown to increase nerve activity in the working muscles, resulting in increased contraction speed of the muscle fibers as well as increases in the amount of force or power output of the muscle.

3. Warming up before exercise may reduce the potential for injury by increasing muscle flexibility. This can assist in the reduction of strains and tears in the muscles and connective tissues.

4. An athlete's blood pressure naturally rises at the beginning of exercise. Warming up before exercise can prevent a *sharp* rise in blood pressure and thus place less stress on the athlete's heart. This can be important to an athlete who might already have high blood pressure, as well as to all athletes who are concerned about their personal health.

5. Overall, research has shown that performance can increase in athletes who warm up before exercise.

A short series of dynamic warm-up exercises is assigned in each of the three workout levels. The dynamic warm-ups are provided in three lists (see chapter 6). The purpose of these warm-up exercises is to improve range of motion using controlled movement patterns similar to those used when playing a sport. Along with improving range of motion, these dynamic movements improve balance and functional strength.

When you begin your daily Jumpmetrics routine, you should go through the assigned dynamic warm-up (identified in the "Warm-up" column of the grid). The dynamic warm-up is a series of functional exercises that improve the flexibility of muscle and the range of joint motion through three planes of motion. These exercises also improve balance and postural and core strength. Each routine should take only a few minutes, but it's highly important to concentrate on the form of each exercise assigned. Focusing on your exercise technique is essential throughout the Jumpmetrics plan. Imagine what your form must look like from someone else's perspective. This concentration on form will begin the motor programming process that will teach your muscles correct posture and position.

Physical Therapy and Flexibility

The physical therapy and flexibility portion of the workout ("PT and flex" column on the grid) gives you an opportunity to work on the areas that gave you problems during the screening from chapter 2. You do not have to work on all of the exercises shown in the grid—only those that you are having problems with. After you complete the dynamic warm-up, take a few minutes to perform the exercises from the screening that gave you the most trouble. Some athletes may feel the need to perform some static muscle stretches before beginning the routine to loosen up. After your PT work, you can lightly stretch, but you may want to wait to perform all the static stretches at one time as a constructive cool-down after practice. The static stretches are performed by holding the stretched position for 15 to 30 seconds. Static stretching techniques promote more permanent length changes in the muscles. However, static stretches can also lead to muscle fatigue and instability—an undesirable side effect before practice.

Certain flexibility exercises have been suggested in chapter 6. These are the physical therapy exercises that help you balance your body's muscle length/tension ratios. Remember that having adequate length/tension relationships between antagonistic muscle groups promotes good joint health. Several flexibility exercises have been included in other sections of the grid that may fit your particular flexibility training needs. These exercises can be performed before practice in the time allotted for the "PT and flex" column of the grids. It is advisable, however, to perform this flexibility exercise more than once during the day, not just during the prepractice routine.

Power

You should move directly to the "Power" portion on the workout grid after you complete the dynamic warm-up (and any of the optional physical therapy and flexibility exercises you choose to do). The power section is designed to provide incremented amounts of plyometric work. This will improve the reactivity or "spring" of the muscle. Plyometric exercises improve power by improving the natural reflex abilities of the muscles. In the level 1 program, the power section is very low in intensity. The intensity of the level 2 and 3 programs is increased. The power section of the workout is a combination of the exercises described in chapters 3 and 4. The core strengthening exercises described in chapter 3 produce powerful hips. Having powerful hips is an asset to power production.

Balance

Once you complete all of the assigned exercises in the power section of the workout, you should immediately begin the exercises in the "Balance" column of the grid. Balance is a critical athletic ability. Correct posture is important to strengthen those muscles used to stabilize and properly align the joints. Balance training is an excellent method of training these smaller stabilizing muscles. Exercises that heavily engage the primary movers (e.g., the quadriceps and hamstrings) often override and minimize the involvement of the stabilizing muscles.

Strength and Overload

Strength is highly important in all areas of athletic performance. If an athlete improves her muscular function and mass, she will have better joint stability and display greater speed and power during performance. Athletes usually participate in a strengthening program regardless of whether they do any other type of training. Most high schools and universities offer resistance training programs to their athletes through physical education classes or team-related conditioning routines. Jumpmetrics offers a resistance plan labeled "Overload" in the grid. This three-day-per-week plan is designed to provide a gradual increase in work demands over time. The strength gained from the overload workouts will enhance athletic performance and provide structure for those athletes who have no strength plan of their own. If you have a predesigned team workout, you should still consider performing the exercises listed under the "Strength" heading on the grid. These strength exercises are optional, but they will ensure functional strength gains that are important to help you build strength in areas that are usually neglected.

© SportsChrome USA

The Jumpmetrics resistance plan is key to developing strength that is important to being a successful athlete.

The exercises in the "Strength" column should be done after your team's practice session. Most of these exercises are performed using only your body weight as resistance. Body weight is a sufficient load for postpractice work due to the levels of fatigue incurred during practice. Using minimal equipment to create strength is also a benefit because this fits most teams' budget and availability of resources.

The "Overload" portion of the grid refers you to the resistance training workouts that are supplemental to each grid. These "Weekly Strength Programs" are performed three days per week, and they are used to ensure that you reach your optimal level of strength for improved performance. The strength programs include exercises described in chapters 3 and 5. Descriptions of additional exercises used in the programs are provided later in this chapter.

Weekly Strength Program Exercises

Lateral reach (see description in chapter 5, page 98)

For complete descriptions of the following exercises, refer to chapter 3.

- One-leg bridge with foot on floor
- One-leg bridge with foot on big ball
- One-leg bridge with hip twist
- One-leg squat with ankle tuck
- One-leg squat with leg out front
- One-leg squat with jump
- Around the world (circuit)
- Bench hamstrings
- Backward lunge
- Baby squats

- Alternating leg lunge
- One-leg Romanian dead lift
- Burpee/squat jump
- Slow low step slide with ankle tether
- Hip circuit #1
- Hip circuit #2
- Lateral unders and step overs
- Tether with internal lunge
- Musketeer lunge
- Static squat
- Slide board

Arm Sprints

Keeping the arms at 90-degree angles, begin moving the arms at the shoulders (and slightly at the elbows) in an alternating fashion as if running in place without moving the legs. The tempo of the movement can begin slowly and then increase. The hands should assume an arch from the "pockets" to cheeks.

Bench Press

Lie on your back on a bench and plant your feet firmly on the floor. Grip the bar with your hands shoulder-width apart and support the bar at arm's length. Lower the bar to your chest with elbows out, then press the bar up by extending the arms.

One-Leg Calf Raise

This version of the heel raise is performed with one leg at a time, using only your body weight for resistance. Keep the knee as straight as possible, using only your ankle to move your weight.

Calf Raise Leg Press

Perform a heel raise on a leg press machine. Allow the toes to rest on the bottom edge of the leg press platform, with the heels hanging off. *Do not turn the platform supports out of their locked position.* If the platform were to slip off the toes, serious injury could occur.

Crabbing

Assume a push-up position, but spread the arms and legs wide apart. Move the left arm and leg out to the side at the same time. Shifting your weight to the left, then move your right arm and leg to the left. Repeat this pattern, thus walking the body along the floor for a given distance.

Dumbbell Lunge With Side Dumbbell Raise

Holding a dumbbell in each hand, step forward performing an alternating leg lunge. Push back from the lunge to a standing position and perform a side dumbbell raise. Remember to keep the elbows and the wrists level with one another during the raise. One set can be performed with the same leg stepping to the front, and then a second set can be performed with the opposite leg stepping out.

Dumbbell Push Press

Assume a standing position with the dumbbells resting at shoulder level. Keep the feet firmly planted shoulder-width apart. Begin by quickly bending the knees about two to three inches. This allows the dumbbells to gain a downward momentum. Then, just as rapidly, extend the knees and at the same time press the dumbbells upward by extending the arms to a point directly over and just slightly behind the head. Then lower the dumbbells under control to their starting position.

Dumbbell Side Lunge With Upright Row

This dumbbell exercise involves the side lunge movement followed by the upright row movement. Perform a side lunge to the left and then to the right before returning to a standing position in the middle to perform the dumbbell upright row.

Dumbbell Split Snatch

This is a full-body exercise. Position the feet just inside shoulder-width apart. Hold a dumbbell in each hand, and begin by pulling one dumbbell close to and up the front of the body. Keep the elbow higher than the wrist during the pull. When the dumbbell reaches shoulder level, jump under the weight by splitting the legs to the front and back. While jumping under the weight, you must rapidly extend the arm so that the dumbbell is extended fully overhead. All of this occurs in one single move. Lower the dumbbell back to the waist and return the legs to their starting position to complete the movement.

Dumbbell Squat With Curl and Press

Perform a dumbbell squat *(a)*. The dumbbells are held at arm's length by your sides. When you stand up from the squat, curl the dumbbells upward toward your chin using your biceps *(b)*. Then press the weights upward above the head to arm's length *(c)*. If the legs are used to help perform the press above the head, it becomes a dumbbell push press instead of a simple dumbbell press. However, this may be necessary if the weight becomes heavy as a result of fatigue.

French Press

While sitting or standing, grasp one dumbbell by the end and extend it above the head at arm's length. It is safer to use fixed dumbbells for this exercise. Removable collars may detach and cause injury. Lower the dumbbell until the lower end of the dumbbell is even with the ears, and then return the dumbbell to the starting position. Keep the elbows close to the head at all times.

Hammer Curl

Perform this arm curl by holding the hand in an anatomically neutral position (as if holding a hammer) and flexing the elbow to bring the dumbbell toward the shoulder. To emphasize the stress placed on the biceps muscle, raise the elbow slightly during the movement. Alternate arms as you go.

Hammer Curl (Walking Rack)

Perform this arm curl by holding the hand in an anatomically neutral position (as if holding a hammer) and flexing the elbow to bring the dumbbell toward the shoulder. To emphasize the stress placed on the biceps muscle, raise the elbow slightly during the movement. Alternate arms when performing these curls. After a given number of repetitions is performed with each arm, pick up a lighter dumbbell and perform the designated repetitions again. The number of weight drops is determined before the set begins.

Hang Clean With Jerk

While holding a weighted bar at full arm's length near your waist, stand with your feet shoulder-width apart (*a*). Begin the movement by rapidly curling the bar upward toward your chin. At the same moment, lightly but rapidly jump from the floor and land in a one-quarter to one-half squat position (*b*). This act of squatting will help you get under the rising bar and make it easier to chamber the bar on your upper chest. Once the bar has stopped and is paused at your upper chest, push your elbows upward to keep the bar's weight from pulling you forward toward the floor. Then stand up while holding the bar in the up position (*c*). Next, rapidly flex and then extend the knee to create an opportunity for change of direction momentum. This momentum

will help you with the next action of pushing the bar upward to full arm's length above your head (*d*). As you push, think of pushing the bar slightly backward behind the line of your ears. This will ensure a safer posture and avoid over-extension of the lower back. After the weight is fully pressed overhead, lower the bar back to its starting point by first returning it to your upper chest. Lean back slightly to decelerate the weight as it returns to your waist at arm's length to complete the movement.

Inch Worm

Perform the inch worm by assuming a push-up position. Keeping the hands stationary, begin walking the feet toward the hands. Use only the movement of the ankles to advance the feet, and keep the legs perfectly straight. Once the feet can progress no farther, begin walking the hands as far out in front of you as you can (beyond the push-up posture). Attempt to keep the lower back from arching toward the floor.

Hop on One Foot or Two Feet

This is a simple hop on and off of either one or two feet. Repeat for the designated times.

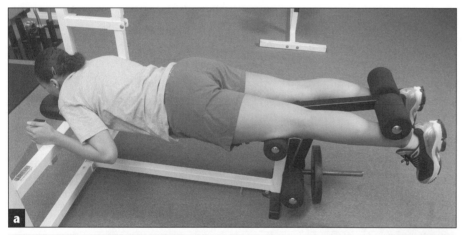

Leg Curl

This exercise can be performed either in a lying or seated position using a leg curl machine (*a*). Flexing the knees, bring the heels toward the buttock (*b*). If lying, attempt to keep the hips firmly against the bench to provide maximum muscle contraction in the hamstrings.

Leg Drag

If on a slick surface such as a basketball court or tile floor, you can place the feet on a towel or seat cushion. Dollies with wheels work well on rough surfaces. With the feet prepared, assume the up position of a push-up. Begin walking along the floor with the hands to a designated point, dragging the legs behind. The legs will sway from left to right with each hand placement. This will work the hips and lower back during the exercise.

Leg Extension

Either with one leg or both legs moving at the same time, fully extend the knee (or knees) using the upper thigh muscles (quadriceps). Pause just briefly, and then slowly lower the weight back to its starting point.

Leg Press

This exercise can be performed with one or two legs. Some machines are made to provide iso-lateral motion and are safer when performing leg presses with one leg. Solid platform leg press machines can be used, but you may choose not to turn the platform supports out of their locked position—this will prevent the platform from coming too far down and trapping the non-working leg. To perform the two-leg version of the press, place the feet flat and firmly in the middle of the platform. Turn the toes slightly outward. Push the weight to full leg extension, and turn the platform supports to their unlocked position. Begin to lower the weight by flexing the knees to a point

where the upper and lower leg form a right angle. To complete the movement, extend the knees to push the platform back to its starting position. For the one-leg version of the press, place the foot in the same position on the platform that it would be if you were doing a two-leg version of the press. Let the free leg occupy the space between the slides, or keep it tucked up and close to your abdominal muscles, to provide safety in case the platform comes down too fast.

Lying Arm Circles

Depending on your shoulder range of motion, this exercise can be performed on a large exercise ball, a bench, or on the floor. If your shoulder range of motion is limited and you feel a pinching or aching while in this position on the floor, then move to a bench or exercise ball. This allows the arms more clearance from the floor, thus lessening the contraction of the rear shoulder muscles. Lie on your belly with the arms clear of the floor and fully extended to the side. Begin performing small circles with the arms. Circles can be performed both forward and backward. If on the floor or a bench, the feet can be held clear of the floor as well to work the middle and lower back.

Medicine Ball Circuit

This is a series of movements with a medicine ball performed one after the other in a circuit fashion.

1. The first is a wood-chopping movement. Start with the ball extended above the head at arm's length *(a)*. The ball is then brought to a point between the legs just above the floor, using a squatting motion *(b)*. The back should remain straight and the chin tilted slightly upward. Perform 10 to 15 repetitions.

2. The second exercise is a large circular rotation performed with the ball. Start with the ball extended above the head at arm's length *(a)*. The ball is then brought down and to your right in a clockwise motion *(c)*. As the ball reaches the far right, begin to squat, bringing the ball to just above the floor. Again, the back should remain straight and the chin tilted slightly upward. The circle continues then to your left as you move up and out of the squat. The movement completes one repetition as the arms complete the circle and end at full extension above the head once more. Perform 10 to 15 repetitions both clockwise and counterclockwise.

3. The third exercise in the circuit is the sideways version of the woodchopper. Begin with the ball extended at arm's length above and to the far left of the head *(d)*. The ball is then brought to a point outside the right ankle just above the floor, using a squatting motion *(e)*. The back should again remain straight and the chin tilted slightly upward. The repetition is completed when the ball is moved up and back to its starting point. Perform 10 to 15 repetitions from upper left to lower right and from upper right to lower left.

This circuit is a great lower and upper body combination exercise, but you will feel it profoundly in the shoulder area.

Pull-Ups

Grasp a pull-up bar with an underhanded grip. Cross your legs behind you and pull your body up until your chin reaches the bar. Return to the starting position.

Power Pull

Start with a barbell at arm's length in front of the hips. Bend the knees two to three inches, allowing the bar to gain a downward momentum (*a*). Straighten the knees and rise up on the toes (as shown) and at the same time begin pulling the bar upward as if to shrug the shoulders (*b*). It is important that the arms remain straight. Because the weight is heavier, it is safer to allow the knees to bend slightly as the bar descends. The bar can then be caught on the upper thighs; this prevents the lower back from having to fully decelerate the weight. Stand straight up again and repeat the process.

Push Press

Assume a standing position with the barbell resting at shoulder level *(a)*. Keep the feet firmly planted shoulder-width apart. Begin by quickly bending the knees about two to three inches. This allows the barbell to gain a downward momentum. Then, just as rapidly, extend the knees and at the same time press the barbell upward by extending the arms to a point directly over and just slightly behind the head *(b)*. Then lower the barbell under control to the starting position.

Side Dumbbell Raise

This exercise can be performed either standing or sitting. Sitting versions of any upper body exercise allow for less lower body involvement, resulting in greater upper body exertion. If standing, begin with the dumbbells at arm's length in front of the lower torso; if sitting, begin with dumbbellsstraight down to the sides of the seat. Keep a very slight bend in the elbows throughout the movement to reduce stress on the elbow joint. Slowly raise the dumbbells upward and out to arm's length at the sides of the body. The palms should remain facing the floor throughout the movement. Once parallel to the floor, the dumbbells should be slightly in front of the body where they can be seen in your peripheral vision. To finish the movement, slowly turn the dumbbells forward so that the thumb on each hand faces downward (as if pouring water from a pitcher). Slowly return the weights to their starting point.

Push-Ups

Support your fully extended body on outstretched arms. The lower back is of primary concern during the movement. To prevent the lower back from arching, keep the abdominal muscles tight and roll the hips forward. The lower back should remain flat during the entire range of motion. Keeping the head slightly up, lower the chest toward the floor. The hands should be in line with the armpits when reaching the bottom position. Return to the up position to complete the movement.

Runner's Rear Deltoid

This exercise can be performed on a large exercise ball or bench. Lie on your belly with the arms bent at 90-degree angles and clear of the floor. Holding the elbows close to the sides and the upper arms parallel to the floor, lift the arms up toward the ceiling. Complete the movement by returning the arm to its parallel position. Because this movement has a short range of motion, a heavier weight can be used.

Runner's Leg Curl

Stand behind a chair and tether your foot with a resisted cable or elastic band via an ankle strap to the front leg of the chair. Flex the heel toward the buttocks. To optimize hamstring involvement, attempt to keep the knee pointing downward and perpendicular to the floor.

Squat

Assume a standing position inside a squat rack with your feet shoulder-width apart and your toes turned slightly out. Take the weight from the stand, look straight ahead at a point on the facing wall, and descend by flexing at the knees. Keep the back completely straight so that the spine is in a natural alignment. Sit back as you descend so that the buttocks are moving to a point well behind the heels. This will keep the shins in a position perpendicular to the floor and prevent the knees from extending too far over the toes. Choose your depth—you can go to a point where your hamstrings are parallel to the floor, or you can go all the way down until your buttocks touch your heels. Be sure not to bounce off the bottom of the squat. To finish the movement, return upward to a standing position, bringing the hips slightly forward to place the back in perfect alignment.

V Push-Ups

Assume a push-up position, and then without moving or sliding the hands on the floor, push down and allow your buttocks to rise. Drop the head toward the floor. Return the body to the push-up position to complete the movement. (This is similar to the downward facing dog in yoga, but the heels aren't flat on the floor.)

Ys and Ts

Depending on your shoulder range of motion, this exercise can be performed on a large exercise ball, a bench, or on the floor. If your shoulder range of motion is limited and you feel a pinching or aching while in this position on the floor, then move to a bench or exercise ball. This allows the arms more clearance from the floor, thus lessening the contraction of the rear shoulder muscles. Lie on your stomach, keeping the elbows straight and the thumbs up, and slowly raise your arms upward and parallel to the floor. Keep the shoulder blades together during the movement. Ys are performed with the arms slightly out in front and to the sides, and Ts are performed with the arms out to the sides.

Nasty Circuit

This circuit consists of a series of four exercises, all done in a push-up position.

Mountain Climbers

From a fully extended push-up position, with the hands shoulder-width apart and under the torso, place one knee at the chest with the toe on the ground. The opposite leg remains fully extended back. Rapidly alternate legs from extension to flexion. Perform for 30 seconds.

Prone Jacks

From a fully extended push-up position, jump the legs apart and then back together, as if performing jumping jacks. The hands stay firmly positioned on the floor (shoulder-width apart and under the torso). Perform for 30 seconds.

Bye Ya

From a fully extended push-up position, lift the legs from the floor one at a time as high as possible without extending the lower back. The hands stay firmly positioned on the floor (shoulder-width apart and under the torso). Perform for 30 seconds.

Hands Up

From a fully extended push-up position, lift the hands from the floor one at a time. The body can twist as the hands are lifted. The elbows can bend, or they can remain fully extended to add additional weight to the turn. Hold for 30 seconds.

Cylinder Circuits

The cylinder circuits are a series of exercises that work the muscles that completely surround and support your spine and hips (cylinder of muscle)—from your upper hips to just below your rib cage.

Cylinder Circuit #1

1. Clock work
2. Hip-up
3. Jackhammer
4. Sit-ups
5. Hanging abs
6. Elbow holds or pull-ins
7. Lean backs
8. Roll-ups

Cylinder Circuit #2

1. Side push-up
2. Reverse sit-up
3. Split jackhammer
4. Quarter sit-up
5. Alternating reverse hyperextension
6. Get-ups
7. Leg writing
8. Roll-outs

Cylinder Circuit #3

1. Hip-up
2. Reverse sit-up
3. Jackhammer
4. Roll-outs
5. Elbow holds or pull-ins
6. Sit-ups
7. Clock work
8. Split jackhammer

Clock Work

Lying on your back, spread your arms straight out to your sides on the floor. Start with your legs held together straight above your hips (*a*). Move your legs side to side, keeping both arms on the floor. Imagine your body as the points on a clock. Your head is at 12:00, and your buttocks are at 6:00. When the legs are moved to the side, they should point toward 3:00 and 9:00 in order to maximize the exercise (*b*).

Hip-Up

Hold a support such as the bottom side of a heavy bench or exercise machine with the hands, or place the hands on the floor at your sides to make the exercise more difficult. Keep the legs straight. Raise the hips off the ground and then slowly lower them (figure at lower left). Make sure to push the legs slightly away from your face (rather than allowing the hips to roll back). This will allow the feet to go back over the head to make the exercise more effective. Exhale during muscle contraction.

Jackhammer

From a sitting position place the hands on the floor behind you with the palms flat and the fingers pointing away from the body. Bring the knees to the chest. Lean back and push the legs away until the feet are just above the floor. Return the knees to the chest to complete the movement. Exhale during muscle contraction.

Sit-Ups

Place the hands behind the head. With the knees bent, anchor the feet under a stable object, such as an exercise machine, or have a partner hold your feet. This exercise will affect the hip flexor muscles as well as the abdominal muscles. Curl the upper body up using the muscles of the abdomen until the elbows come past the knees. Lower the upper body downward until the lower to midback touches the floor. This completes the repetition. Exhale during muscle contraction.

Hanging Abs (Hanging Knee-Up)

Hang from a chin-up bar. Pull the knees upward and hold long enough to exhale your breath at the top of the movement. You can perform these in a supported fashion with your feet touching the ground every time, or you can hang so the feet do not touch (thus requiring more body control).

Elbow Holds or Pull-Ins

Leaning on the elbows, assume a push-up position. Placing most of the body's weight on the elbows, force the chin out beyond the hands. Hold this position for 30 seconds or more to perform the postural hold. Make certain that the lower back is in a neutral or flat position. Allowing the lower back to arch toward the floor is counterproductive to the exercise.

Another variation of this exercise is the pull-in. From the previously described elbow posture, begin contracting the abdominal muscles as if to do a sit-up. Exhale during the contraction. This will assure the full effect of the movement. This sit-up variation can be performed by itself or, for a greater challenge, at the end of the postural holds.

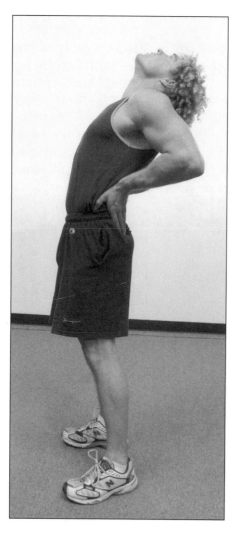

Lean Backs

This exercise is a standing sit-up, coming up from a bent back posture. The farther you can lean back, the more you will feel the movement in the abdominal muscles. In the beginning, before postural strength is developed, this exercise will be very stressful on the lower back, so use it sparingly. Over time this exercise will provide great functional strength. From a standing position, place the feet wider than shoulder-width apart. Place the hands on the hips. Lean back as far as you comfortably can, and then use the abdominal muscles to pull yourself back to a standing position. Exhale during muscle contraction.

Roll-Ups

Place the feet on a movable object (a large exercise ball or a dolly with wheels). Place the hands on the floor in a push-up position. Begin the movement by using the abdominal muscles to initiate the movement of the hips, drawing the knees toward the chest. Return the legs to the fully extended position to complete the movement. Exhale during muscle contraction.

Side Push-Up

Lie on your side with one foot on top of the other. Use the feet as a fulcrum. Place the forearm of the down (underside) arm flat on the floor, and place the hand of the opposite arm in front of the belly or on your hip and on its fingertips. Lift the hips straight up, using the arms for support. Variations of this exercise can be done by turning the body more inward so that more of the belly is facing the ground. This will shift the emphasis from the side or oblique muscles to the intercostals around the front rib cage. Exhale during muscle contraction.

Reverse Sit-Up

Using the arms for support, bring the knees to the chin. Lift the buttocks from the floor. Then slowly lower the buttocks while at the same time straightening and pushing the legs away. The legs should be nearly straight and as low to the floor as possible while still keeping your lower back in contact with the floor. As you become stronger in the lower abdominals, you will be able to lower the legs farther from the floor. Exhale during muscle contraction.

Split Jackhammer

Perform this exercise like the jackhammer, but bring the knees to the chest one at a time, allowing the other leg to remain fully extended. Exhale during muscle contraction.

Quarter Sit-Up

Bend the legs slightly while hovering the feet two inches from the ground. This creates a natural arch in the lower back. Flatten the arch into the floor by lifting the hips up and contracting the abdominals. Exhale during muscle contraction.

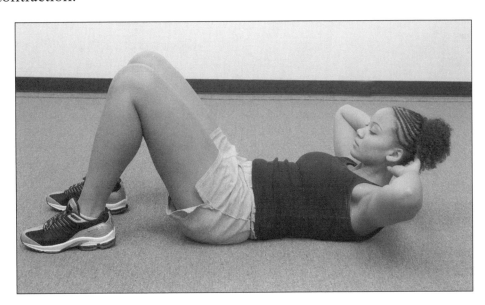

Alternating Reverse Hyperextension

Lie facedown on a tall table or bench and grasp the edges of the table firmly with both hands. The feet should hang down toward the floor. Begin the movement by raising the legs up one at a time until parallel with the floor.

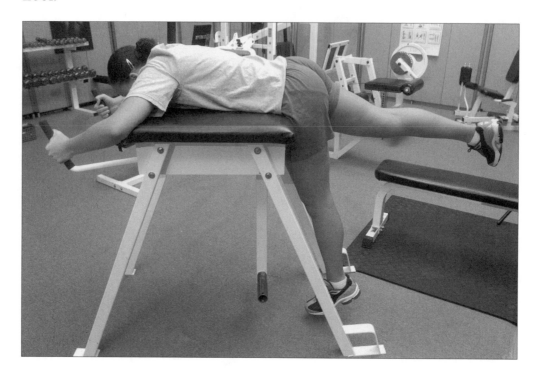

Get-Ups

Lie on your back on the floor with your knees bent and pulled up toward the chest *(a)*. As fast as you can, sit up, and using your hands, jump up to a full standing position *(b, c)*. Then quickly return to a full lying position to complete the movement. *Warning: Rapid changes of position can sometimes cause light-headedness. Therefore, perform this exercise in an open area free of clutter or exercise equipment in case fainting occurs.*

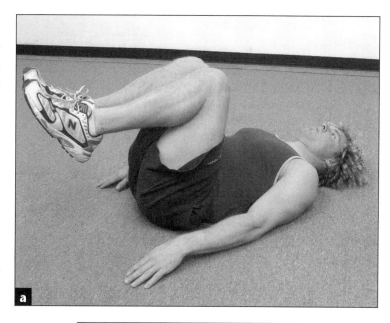

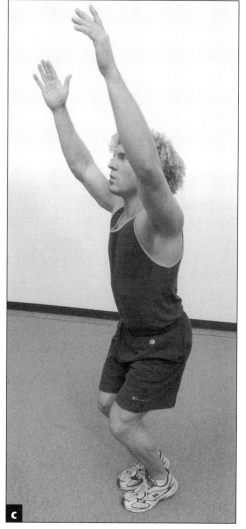

Leg Writing

In a sitting position, lean slightly back and support yourself with your hands on the floor. Raise the legs from the floor while keeping them perfectly straight. Begin tracing the letters of the alphabet (large capital letters) in the air with your feet. Do not bend your knees; use only your hips to move the legs. As your feet go up, your upper body should come up from the floor (forming a V with your body). As your legs go down, you should allow your upper body to go down in order to control the weight of your legs. Write as many letters as you can. Each time you repeat the exercise, add more letters.

Roll-Outs

Assume a position on the floor on your knees. Using a dolly with wheels, an exercise wheel, or even a spool for coaxial cable with a center dowel, place your hands on the movable object and roll the object away from you, thus lowering your chest and hips to the floor. Keep the arms in front of you and as straight as possible. Placing a firm downward pressure on the movable object, begin rolling the object back toward you, returning to the starting position.

8

Level 1 Program

The Jumpmetrics workout plans provide a hierarchy of training intensity and complexity. Level 1 is the least complex of the three workout plans; however, it should be performed by all athletes regardless of the score they achieved on the Jumpmetrics evaluation. It is essential that all athletes receive the basic postural training that level 1 provides. Although the training in level 1 may seem basic, it is often difficult for even the most experienced athlete to get the arms and legs working together as a unit and maintain the proper body position at the same time. After you complete all of the training levels, you may want to return and retry level 1 training again. Even though some exercises will feel easier than they did the first time through, you may find some to be just as challenging because they require a more basic movement pattern that is contrary to the complex movement patterns you have grown accustomed to. The level 1 through 3 workouts are only stair steps. To benefit from the use of a set of stairs, you must go up and down the stairs to get to where you are going. The same is true here—you must experience the levels and then reexperience them to understand the subtleties of your own body movements when performing the exercises.

The level 1 program introduces the athlete to postures and positions that ensure safety and improve force production. This is a teaching level, so the intensity and complexity of the exercises in this level are low. Jumping exercises found in level 1 training are performed on both legs with a focus on position and posture during landings and takeoffs. Exercises are performed in place or with minimal distance traveled. Plyometric jumps are performed low to the floor. Change of direction is limited to side-to-side, two-foot jumping (for hip and knee stability).

165

The primary emphasis for the level 1 athlete is to improve posture during landing and takeoff. Postural improvements require improvements in muscular strength and neuromuscular control. Body weight resistance and weight training exercises are assigned to produce an overload effect for increasing strength. Teaching the muscles to fire in the correct pattern (neuromuscular control) is achieved through balance training and correctly jumping and landing in a variety of positions. Correct jumping and landing form can be ensured through proper cueing from a coach or teammates.

Balance exercises in this level are performed on one leg to ensure that equal strength is developed in both legs. One-leg exercises are important in the development of balance and neuromuscular control. Performing on one leg works the deeper stabilizing muscles of the hips that ultimately control the alignment of the knees.

When jumping and landing in level 1, the landing postures are statically held (holding the landing in place for a few seconds without moving). Holding the landing is counterintuitive to athletic performance because an athlete never has time to hold a landing during the playing of a sport. Holding the posture allows the athlete to evaluate the position of the knee and to gain a sense of position. When reinforced through the habit of static holds, proper posture will occur regardless of the speed of movement. Holding the posture will also help to increase muscular strength that can aid in stabilizing the joints.

The level 1 program is performed for 12 sessions. These sessions can be performed each practice, so the athlete can complete level 1 training in three weeks. Athletes who respond poorly and need more time in level 1 can repeat the cycle before advancing.

Level 1 Weekly Strength Program

The level 1 weekly strength program starting on page 169 primarily uses body weight resistance exercises. If an athlete can gain initial control of her own body weight before moving on to more traditional weight training exercises, she will perform the weight training exercises with less difficulty. The level 1 weekly strength program includes two separate workouts to provide variety and to increase exercise complexity and intensity over time. Each workout is performed for two weeks before moving forward to the next workout plan. Staying with the workout for more than one week will ensure that the exercises are learned completely and that the body has an opportunity to strengthen itself against the stresses of the exercises. The level 1 workouts are performed on weeks 1 through 4 of the total Jumpmetrics plan.

Level 1 JUMPMETRICS Exercise Progression

DAY	Warm-Up	PT and flex (optional)	Power	Balance	Strength (optional postpractice)	Overload
1	Perform dynamic list 1 (refer to table 6.1)	**Screening exercises** Perform 10 repetitions of the screening exercises you had difficulty with.	a. Jump rope (two feet) 1 × 75 *Hold landings for 5 seconds on the following:* b. Broad jump 1 × 10 c. Vertical jump 1 × 10 d. Lateral bounce 1 × 10	*Perform the following for 30 seconds on each foot (shoes off):* a. One-quarter squat on one foot b. Half squat on one foot	a. Static squat 2 × 1 minute b. Tether with internal lunge 2 × 30 (each leg)	**Refer to Level 1 Weekly Strength Program**
2	Perform dynamic list 1	*Refer to chapter 2 for explanations of the exercises. Always focus on proper knee position on jumps and landings.*	a. Zigzag jump (small) 1 × 10 *(Hold landings for 5 seconds.)* b. Sock twist (15 yards and back)	*Perform the following for 30 seconds on each foot (shoes off):* a. Quarter turn b. Half turn	*Perform the following on each leg:* a. One-leg bridge with foot on floor 2 × 30 seconds b. One-leg squat 2 × 10 (using hands for support)	
3	Perform dynamic list 1	• Single-leg squat • Jumping and landing with good form • Single-leg hops • Bridge	a. Ankle bounce (two feet) 2 × 25 *Hold landings for 5 seconds on the following:* b. Hexagon drill 2 × 1 minute c. Tuck jump 1 × 10	*Perform the following for 30 seconds on each foot (shoes off):* a. One-foot balance with head turn (left and right) b. One-foot balance with eyes closed	a. Alternating leg lunge (15 yards and back) b. Step slide (15 yards and back) c. Musketeer lunge (15 yards and back) d. Hip circuit #2	
4	Perform dynamic list 1	**Flexibility exercises** *Refer to chapter 2 to perform your assigned flexibility exercises.*	a. Jump rope (two feet) 1 × 100 *Hold landings for 5 seconds on the following:* b. Broad jump 1 × 12 c. Vertical jump 1 × 12 d. Lateral bounce 1 × 12	One-leg quarter squat with medicine ball toss (2 minutes each foot; shoes off)	a. Static squat 3 × 1 minute b. Lateral reach 2 × 10 (perform on each leg)	
5	Perform dynamic list 1	Big toe Calves/ankles Quadriceps Hamstrings Hip flexors Iliotibial band (ITB) Hip external rotators Hip internal rotators Shoulders and upper back	a. Zigzag jump (small) 1 × 12 *(Hold landings for 5 seconds.)* b. Sock twist (20 yards and back)	Quarter-turn back kick (30 seconds each foot; shoes off)	*Perform the following on each leg:* a. One-leg Romanian dead lift 2 × 15 b. Lateral unders 2 × 15	
6	Perform dynamic list 1		a. Ankle bounce (two feet) 2 × 25 *Hold landings for 5 seconds on the following:* b. Hexagon drill 2 × 1 minute c. Tuck jump 1 × 12	Hop stick landing (30 yards and back)	a. Backward lunge (15 yards and back) b. Step slide (15 yards and back) c. Musketeer lunge (15 yards and back) d. Hip circuit #1	

(continued)

Level 1 JUMPMETRICS Exercise Progression *(continued)*

DAY	Warm-Up	PT and flex (optional)	Power	Balance	Strength (optional postpractice)	Overload
7	Perform dynamic list 2	**Screening exercises** Perform 10 repetitions of the screening exercises you had difficulty with.	a. Jump rope (two feet) 1 × 100 *Hold landings for 5 seconds on the following:* b. Broad jump 1 × 14 c. Vertical jump 1 × 14 d. Lateral bounce 1 × 14	*Perform the following for 1 minute on each foot (shoes off):* a. Half squat (knee wiper) b. Quarter turn c. Four point touch	a. Baby squats 2 × 1 minute (1 squat per second) b. Tether with internal lunge 3 × 30 (each leg)	**Refer to Level 1 Weekly Strength Program**
8	Perform dynamic list 2	*Refer to chapter 2 for explanations of the exercises. Always focus on proper knee position on jumps and landings.*	a. Zigzag jump (small) 1 × 14 *(Hold landings for 5 seconds.)* b. Sock twist (15 yards and back)	*Perform the following for 1 minute on each foot (shoes off):* a. Quarter turn with perturbations b. Half turn	*Perform the following on each leg:* a. One-leg bridge with foot on floor 2 × 30 seconds b. One-leg squat with ankle tuck 2 × 10	
9	Perform dynamic list 2	• Single-leg squat • Jumping and landing with good form • Single-leg hops • Bridge	a. Ankle bounce (two feet) 2 × 25 *Hold landings for 5 seconds on the following:* b. Hexagon drill 3 × 1 minute c. Tuck jump 1 × 14	One-foot balance with medicine ball toss (2 minutes each foot; shoes off)	a. Alternating leg lunge (15 yards and back) b. Step slide (15 yards and back) c. Musketeer lunge (15 yards and back) d. Hip circuit #2	
10	Perform dynamic list 2	**Flexibility exercises** *Refer to chapter 2 to perform your assigned flexibility exercises.*	a. Jump rope (two feet) 1 × 100 *Hold landings for 5 seconds on the following:* b. Broad jump 1 × 16 c. Vertical jump 1 × 16 d. Lateral bounce 1 × 16	*Perform the following for 1 minute on each foot (shoes off):* a. One-foot balance with head turn (left and right) b. Half squat (knee wiper) c. Four point touch	a. Baby squats 3 × 1 minute (1 squat per second) b. Lateral reach 3 × 10 (each leg)	
11	Perform dynamic list 2	Big toe Calves/ankles Quadriceps Hamstrings Hip flexors Iliotibial band (ITB) Hip external rotators Hip internal rotators Shoulders and upper back	a. Zigzag jump (small) 1 × 16 *(Hold landings for 5 seconds.)* b. Sock twist (30 yards and back)	*Perform the following for 1 minute on each foot (shoes off):* a. Quarter-turn back kick b. Multidirectional kick	a. One-leg Romanian dead lift 2 × 15 (each leg) b. Lateral unders 3 × 15 (each leg) c. Burpee/squat jump 2 × 10	
12	Perform dynamic list 2		a. Ankle bounce (two feet) 2 × 25 *Hold landings for 5 seconds on the following:* b. Hexagon drill 3 × 1 minute c. Tuck jump 1 × 16	a. Hop stick landing with side kick (30 yards and back) b. One-foot fire brigade	a. Backward lunge (15 yards and back) b. Step slide (15 yards and back) c. Musketeer lunge (15 yards and back) d. Hip circuit #1	

JUMPMETRICS

Level 1 Weekly Strength Program

WEEKS 1-2

Monday

One-leg squat	8 × ___ 8 × ___ 8 × ___
Lateral unders or stepovers	10 × ___ 10 × ___
One-leg bridge with hip twist	30 seconds 30 seconds
Musketeer lunge with side kick	10 × ___ 10 × ___
One-leg calf raise	25 × ___ 25 × ___
Around the world	1 ×

Wednesday

Burpees	10 × ___ 10 × ___
Crabbing	15 yards and back 15 yards and back
Lying arm circles	1 minute 1 minute
Medicine ball circuit	1 × ball weight ____
Arm springs	30 seconds 30 seconds

Friday

Pull-ups   10 × ___   10 × ___

(Add 3 negatives if 10 is not obtained. For example, if you are only able to do 9 reps in a set, then get a chair or use the pull-up apparatus to stand on. Put your chin above the bar and then let yourself down very slowly. Repeat these eccentric or negative pull-ups for 3 additional reps beyond the number you achieved before muscle exhaustion set in.)

Push-ups   10 × ___   10 × ___

(Add 3 negatives if 10 is not obtained)

Baby squats	1 minute 1 minute
Hip circuit #1	1 ×
Bench hamstrings	10 × ___ 10 × ___ 8 × ___
Hop on one foot or two feet	25 × (one foot) 50 × (two feet)
Inch worm	15 yards and back

▶ You must increase weight with each set where resistance is used. The last set is the power set and must increase in weight each week (therefore, do not start too heavy). Increase repetitions where body weight or a weighted vest is used.

JUMPMETRICS

Level 1 Weekly Strength Program

WEEKS 3-4

Monday

Squat	8 × ___	8 × ___	8 × ___
One-leg squat	8 × ___	8 × ___	8 × ___
One-leg bridge with foot on ball		30 seconds	30 seconds
Runner's leg curl	8 × ___	8 × ___	8 × ___
One-leg calf raise		25 × ___	25 × ___
Around the world			2 ×

Wednesday

Dumbbell squat with curl and press	8 × ___	8 × ___
Dumbbell side lunge with upright row	8 × ___	8 × ___
Dumbbell lunge with side dumbbell raise	8 × ___	8 × ___
Medicine ball circuit	1 × ball weight ____	
V push-ups	10 × ___	10 × ___
Ys and Ts	20 × ___	20 × ___

Friday

Burpees		10 × ___	10 × ___
Crabbing		20 yards and back	20 yards and back
Hip circuit #1			1 ×
Bench hamstrings	10 × ___	10 × ___	8 × ___
Hop on one foot or two feet	35 × (one foot)	70 × (two feet)	
Nasty circuit			1 ×

▶ You must increase weight with each set where resistance is used. The last set is the power set and must increase in weight each week (therefore, do not start too heavy). Increase repetitions where body weight or a weighted vest is used.

9

Level 2 Program

The level 2 program elevates the athlete to a slightly higher level of performance. Level 2 introduces one-leg hops that are performed low to the ground. Movements off two legs are performed in place or over a distance. Additional movements include twisting and turning while remaining in one place. Some exercises from the level 1 plan are revisited; however, the number of repetitions or sets of those exercises are increased. Level 2 includes two-foot changes of direction as well as predictable changes of direction off one leg, either moving around or to and from an object. Predictable means that the athlete knows the patterns of motion before the activity begins.

New dynamic warm-up exercises are introduced, as well as a variety of new strength exercises in the optional "Strength" and "Overload" sections of the workout grid. These new exercises are included to ensure that the muscles continue adapting to new stimuli and become stronger. These new exercises also ensure that the athlete remains invested in the program and that enthusiasm remains high.

Like level 1, the level 2 program is performed for 12 sessions. After completing level 1 training, athletes should perform the Jumpmetrics evaluation again. The athlete should achieve a score of 3 on each of the first five tests of the evaluation. If the athlete performs less than perfect on these tests, it is suggested that he repeat the level 1 program. (The athlete may still be unable to receive a top score in the hamstring curl and the bridge.) If the athlete makes the desired score on the first five tests, he can proceed to level 2 training on the next scheduled exercise day. Each level 2 workout can be performed (in the order presented) before practice. At the end of the 12 sessions, if the athlete again fails to perform well on the final two exercises in the Jumpmetrics evaluation, the athlete should repeat level 2 training before advancing to the final level.

Level 2 JUMPMETRICS Exercise Progression

DAY	Warm-Up	PT and flex (optional)	Power	Balance	Strength (optional postpractice)	Overload
1	Perform dynamic list 1 (refer to table 6.1)	**Screening exercises** Perform 10 repetitions of the screening exercises you had difficulty with.	a. Two-foot twist hop 1 × 30 yards b. Broad jump 1 × 30 yards c. One-leg long jump 4 × (each leg) d. Ice-skaters 1 × 10 e. Cone ladder 2 × laterally, 2 × forward and back	*Perform the following for 1 minute on each foot (shoes off):* a. One-foot balance b. Quarter turn with perturbations c. Four point touch	a. Slow low step slide with ankle tether (30 yards and back) b. Hip circuit #1 c. Nasty circuit	**Refer to Level 1 Weekly Strength Program**
2	Perform dynamic list 2	*Refer to chapter 2 for explanations of the exercises. Always focus on proper knee position on jumps and landings.*	a. One-foot hop with rotations 1 × 30 yards b. 20-yard shuttle 3 × c. Mogul hops (small) 1 × 10 d. Half-spin jump 10 × each way	*Perform the following for 1 minute on each foot (shoes off):* a. Half turn b. Quarter-turn back kick	*Perform the following on each leg:* a. One-leg bridge with foot on ball 2 × 30 seconds b. One-leg squat with ankle tuck 2 × 10	
3	Perform dynamic list 3	• Single-leg squat • Jumping and landing with good form • Single-leg hops • Bridge	a. Ankle bounce (one foot) 1 × 50 b. Two-legged sideways broad jump (15 yards and back) 1 × 5 c. One-leg vertical takeoff 1 × 10 d. Power skip	*Perform the following for 1 minute on each foot (shoes off):* a. One-foot balance with head turn (left and right) b. Quarter turn c. Four point touch	a. Transverse lunge 2 × 10 b. Hip circuit #2 c. Burpee/squat jump 2 × 10	
4	Perform dynamic list 1	**Flexibility exercises** *Refer to chapter 2 to perform your assigned flexibility exercises.*	a. Lateral hop 1 × 30 yards b. Zigzag run (inside and outside leg) 1 × 30 yards c. Vertical jump 2 × 8 d. Zigzag jump (small) 1 × 10	One-leg balance with medicine ball toss (2 minutes each foot; shoes off)	a. Baby squats 2 × 1 minute (1 squat per second) b. Lateral reach 2 × 10 (perform on each leg)	
5	Perform dynamic list 2	Big toe Calves/ankles Quadriceps Hamstrings Hip flexors Iliotibial band (ITB) Hip external rotators Hip internal rotators Shoulders and upper back	a. Two-foot twist hop 2 × 30 yards b. Broad jump 2 × 30 yards c. One-leg long jump 6 × (each leg) d. Ice-skaters 2 × 10 (each leg) e. Cone ladder 2 × laterally, 2 × forward and back	a. Two-knee balance on ball (2 minutes) b. Multidirectional kick (2 minutes each foot; shoes off)	*Perform the following on each leg:* a. One-leg bridge with hip twist 2 × 30 seconds b. One-leg squat with leg out front 2 × 10	
6	Perform dynamic list 3		a. One-foot hop with rotations 2 × 30 yards b. 20-yard shuttle 4 × c. Mogul hops (small) 2 × 10 d. Half-spin jump 12 × each way	a. Hop stick landing with back stick (30 yards and back) b. One-foot fire brigade	a. Around the world 1 × b. Hip circuit #1 c. Nasty circuit	

DAY	Warm-Up	PT and flex (optional)	Power	Balance	Strength (optional postpractice)	Overload
7	Perform dynamic list 1	**Screening exercises** Perform 10 repetitions of the screening exercises you had difficulty with.	a. Ankle bounce (one foot) 1 × 50 b. Two-legged sideways broad jump (20 yards and back) c. One-leg vertical takeoff 1 × 6 d. Power skip 2 × 10	Perform the following for 30 seconds on each foot (shoes off): a. One-foot balance b. One-quarter squat one one foot c. Half squat on one foot	a. Static squat 2 × 1 minute b. Tether with internal lunge 2 × 30 (each leg)	**Refer to Level 2 Weekly Strength Program**
8	Perform dynamic list 2	Refer to chapter 2 for explanations of the exercises. Always focus on proper knee position on jumps and landings.	a. Lateral hop 2 × 30 yards b. Zigzag run 2 × 30 yards (inside and outside leg) c. Vertical jump 2 × 10 d. Zigzag jump (small) 1 × 10	Perform the following for 30 seconds on each foot (shoes off): a. Quarter turn b. Half turn	Perform the following on each leg: a. One-leg bridge with foot on floor 2 × 30 seconds b. One-leg squat with leg out front 2 × 10	
9	Perform dynamic list 3	• Single-leg squat • Jumping and landing with good form • Single-leg hops • Bridge	a. Two-foot twist hop 1 × 30 yards b. Broad jump 1 × 30 yards c. One-leg long jump 5 × (each leg) d. Ice-skaters 1 × 10 (each leg) e. Cone ladder 2 × laterally, 2 × forward and back	Perform the following for 30 seconds on each foot (shoes off): a. One-foot balance b. One-foot balance with head turn (left and right) c. One-foot balance with eyes closed	a. Alternating leg lunge (15 yards and back) b. Step slide (15 yards and back) c. Musketeer lunge (15 yards and back) d. Hip circuit #2	
10	Perform dynamic list 1	**Flexibility exercises** Refer to chapter 2 to perform your assigned flexibility exercises. Big toe Calves/ankles Quadriceps Hamstrings Hip flexors Iliotibial band (ITB) Hip external rotators Hip internal rotators Shoulders and upper back	a. One-foot hop with rotations 1 × 30 yards b. 20-yard shuttle 5 × c. Mogul hops (small) 1 × 10 d. Half spin jump 10 × each way	One-leg quarter squat with medicine ball toss (2 minutes each foot; shoes off)	a. Baby squats 2 × 1 minute (1 squat per second) b. Lateral reach 2 × 10 (perform on each leg)	
11	Perform dynamic list 2		a. Ankle bounce (one foot) 1 × 50 b. Two-legged sideways broad jump (30 yards and back) c. One-leg vertical takeoff 1 × 10 d. Power skip 1 × 10	Perform the following for 30 seconds on each foot (shoes off): a. Quarter-turn back kick b. Lateral reach	a. One-leg Romanian dead lift 2 × 15 (each leg) b. Lateral unders 2 × 15 (each leg)	
12	Perform dynamic list 3		a. Lateral hop 2 × 30 yards b. Zigzag run 2 × 30 yards (inside and outside leg) c. Vertical jump 3 × 10 d. Zigzag jump (small) 1 × 10	Hop stick landing (30 yards and back)	a. Backward lunge (15 yards and back) b. Step slide (15 yards and back) c. Musketeer lunge (15 yards and back) d. Hip circuit #1	

Exercises from level 1 may be repeated in the level 2 workout grid. The number of sets of the exercises has been increased to challenge the athlete's ability to maintain good form in the movement while feeling fatigued.

Level 2 Weekly Strength Program

The level 2 weekly strength program primarily uses body weight resistance exercises during the first two weeks but begins to add exercises that use dumbbell loaded resistance during the second two weeks. This change provides a level of variety that challenges inactive muscle fibers. The addition of external loading through dumbbells or other added resistance also acts to stimulate inactive muscle cells. Overloading with external resistance makes your body weight seem less heavy by contrast. If you add additional weight to your arms and legs during a workout, you will feel lighter and your movements will become easier when you return to your normal body weight after the workout. The level 2 workouts are performed on weeks 5 through 8 of the total Jumpmetrics plan.

JUMPMETRICS

Level 2 Weekly Strength Program

WEEKS 5-6

Monday

One-leg squat	8 × ___ 8 × ___ 8 × ___
Lateral unders or step overs	10 × ___ 10 × ___
Two-leg bridge on big ball	30 seconds 30 seconds
Musketeer lunge with side kick	10 × ___ 10 × ___
One-leg calf raise	25 × ___ 25 × ___
Around the world	1 ×
Cylinder circuit #1	1 ×

Wednesday

Burpees	10 × ___ 10 × ___
Crabbing	30 yards and back 30 yards and back
Lying arm circles	1 minute 1 minute
Medicine ball circuit	1 × ball weight ___
Runner's rear deltoid	30 seconds 30 seconds
Cylinder circuit #2	1 ×

Friday

Pull-ups	10 × ___ 10 × ___
(Add 3 negatives if 10 is not obtained)	
Push-ups	10 × ___ 10 × ___
(Add 3 negatives if 10 is not obtained)	
Baby squats	1 minute 1 minute
Hip circuit #1	1 ×
Bench hamstrings	10 × ___ 10 × ___ 8 × ___
Hop on one foot or two feet	25 × (one foot) 50 × (two feet)
Inch worm	20 yards and back
Cylinder circuit #3	1 ×

▶ You must increase weight with each set where resistance is used. The last set is the power set and must increase in weight each week (therefore, do not start too heavy). Increase repetitions where body weight or a weighted vest is used.

JUMPMETRICS

Level 2 Weekly Strength Program

Monday

Squat	8 × ___	8 × ___	8 × ___
One-leg squat	8 × ___	8 × ___	8 × ___
One-leg bridge on big ball		30 seconds	30 seconds
Runner's leg curl	8 × ___	8 × ___	8 × ___
One-leg calf raise		25 × ___	25 × ___
Around the world			2 ×
Cylinder circuit #1			1 ×

Wednesday

Dumbbell squat with curl and press	8 × ___	8 × ___
Dumbbell side lunge with upright row	8 × ___	8 × ___
Dumbbell lunge with side dumbbell raise	8 × ___	8 × ___
Medicine ball circuit	1 × ball weight ____	
V push-ups	10 × ___	10 × ___
Ys and Ts	20 × ___	20 × ___
Cylinder circuit #2		1 ×

Friday

Burpees		10 × ___	10 × ___
Crabbing		30 yards and back	30 yards and back
Hip circuit #2			1 ×
Bench hamstrings	10 × ___	10 × ___	8 × ___
Hop on one foot or two feet	35 × (one foot)	70 × (two feet)	
Nasty circuit			1 ×
Cylinder circuit #3			1 ×

▶ You must increase weight with each set where resistance is used. The last set is the power set and must increase in weight each week (therefore, do not start too heavy). Increase repetitions where body weight or a weighted vest is used.

10

Level 3 Program

The level 3 program advances the athlete to the final stage of training. Level 3 introduces one-leg hops performed while twisting in the transverse plane. These twisting actions are performed while moving in various directions. Some exercises from the level 1 and level 2 plans are revisited to reinforce basic motor patterns. Changes of direction in level 3 consist of predictable and unpredictable directional drills. Predictable directional drills involve changes of direction that the athlete is made aware of before the exercise begins (e.g., the athlete knows she will sprint and then cut to the left). Unpredictable changes of direction are not established prior to the exercise. The directions are called out during the exercise. The athletes are expected to perform the skills of moving around an object and moving to and from an object in the correct manner.

The final groups of dynamic warm-up exercises are introduced as well as a variety of new strength exercises in the optional "Strength" and "Overload" sections of the workout grid.

The level 3 program is performed for 18 sessions. The expanded length of the level 3 program adds to the program's intensity.

Level 3 JUMPMETRICS Exercise Progression

DAY	Warm-Up	PT and flex (optional)	Power	Balance	Strength (optional postpractice)	Overload
1	Perform dynamic list 4 (refer to table 6.1)	**Screening exercises** Perform 10 repetitions of the screening exercises you had difficulty with.	a. One-foot twist hop 2 × 150 yards b. One-leg long jump 4 × (each leg) c. Cone pattern 1 × 30 seconds d. Zigzag run 2 × 30 yards (inside and outside leg)	*Perform the following for 1 minute on each foot (shoes off):* a. Half squat (knee wiper) b. Quarter turn c. Four point touch	a. Slow low step slide with ankle tether (30 yards and back) b. Hip circuit #1	**Refer to Level 3 Weekly Strength Program**
2	Perform dynamic list 5	*Refer to chapter 2 for explanations of the exercises. Always focus on proper knee position on jumps and landings.*	a. One-foot hop with rotations 1 × 30 yards b. Three-cone reaction 3 × c. Cycle jump 1 × 30 seconds d. Full-spin jump 5 × each way	*Perform the following for 1 minute on each foot (shoes off):* a. Half turn b. Quarter-turn back kick	*Perform the following on each leg:* a. One-leg bridge with foot on ball 2 × 30 seconds b. One-leg squat with leg out front 2 × 10	
3	Perform dynamic list 6	• Single-leg squat • Jumping and landing with good form • Single-leg hops • Bridge	a. Ankle bounce (one foot) 1 × 50 b. One-leg sideways broad jump (15 yards and back) c. One-leg vertical takeoff 1 × 10 d. Called pattern jumps 3 × 30 seconds	One-foot balance with medicine ball toss (2 minutes each foot; shoes off)	a. Around the world 1 × b. Hip circuit #2 c. One-leg Romanian dead lift 2 × 15	
4	Perform dynamic list 4	**Flexibility exercises** *Refer to chapter 2 to perform your assigned flexibility exercises.* Big toe Calves/ankles Quadriceps Hamstrings Hip flexors Iliotibial band (ITB) Hip external rotators Hip internal rotators Shoulders and upper back	a. Lateral hop 1 × 30 yards b. Zigzag run 1 × 30 yards (inside and outside leg) c. Vertical jump 2 × 8 d. Sprint cutting 3 ×	*Perform the following for 1 minute on each foot (shoes off):* a. One-foot balance with head turn (left and right) b. Half squat (knee wiper) c. Four point touch	a. Baby squats 2 × 1 minute (1 squat per second) b. Lateral reach 2 × 10 (perform on each leg)	
5	Perform dynamic list 5		a. Box reaction 2 × 30 seconds	a. Lateral reach (1 minute on each foot; shoes off) b. Two-knee balance on ball (4 minutes)	*Perform the following on each leg:* a. One-leg bridge with hip twist 2 × 30 seconds b. One-leg squat with leg out front 3 × 10	
6	Perform dynamic list 6		a. Depth jumps (from 12-inch height) 2 × 10 b. Tuck jump 2 × 10 c. Ice-skaters 3 × 30 seconds	Hop stick landing with back stick (30 yards and back)	a. Around the world 1 × b. Hip circuit #1	

DAY	Warm-Up	PT and flex (optional)	Power	Balance	Strength (optional postpractice)	Overload
7	**Perform dynamic list 1**	**Screening exercises** Perform 10 repetitions of the screening exercises you had difficulty with.	a. One-foot twist hop 2 × 15 yards b. One-leg long jump 4 × (each leg) c. Cone pattern 2 × 30 seconds d. Zigzag run 3 × 30 yards (inside and outside leg)	a. Two-knee balance on ball (3 minutes) b. Hop stick landing with side kick (30 yards and back)	a. Nasty circuit 1 × b. Bench hamstrings 3 × 10 c. One-leg Romanian dead lift 2 × 15	**Refer to Level 3 Weekly Strength Program**
8	**Perform dynamic list 2**	*Refer to chapter 2 for explanations of the exercises. Always focus on proper knee position on jumps and landings.*	a. One-foot hop with rotations 2 × 30 yards b. Three-cone reaction 3 × c. Cycle jump 2 × 30 seconds d. Full-spin jump 6 × each way	*Perform the following for 2 minutes on each foot (shoes off):* a. Quarter-turn back kick with ground touch b. Multidirectional kick 2 ×	a. Burpee/squat jump 2 × 10 b. Transverse lunge 2 × 10 c. One-leg squat with leg out front 2 × 10	
9	**Perform dynamic list 3**	• Single-leg squat • Jumping and landing with good form • Single-leg hops • Bridge	a. Ankle bounce (one foot) 1 × 60 b. One-leg sideways broad jump (15 yards and back) c. One-leg vertical takeoff 1 × 12 d. Called pattern jumps 3 × 30 seconds	*Perform the following for 2 minutes on each foot (shoes off):* a. One-foot balance with eyes closed b. Quarter turn with perturbations	a. Slow low step slide with ankle tether (30 yards and back) b. Hip circuit #2	
10	**Perform dynamic list 4**	**Flexibility exercises** *Refer to chapter 2 to perform your assigned flexibility exercises.*	a. Lateral hop 1 × 30 yards b. Zigzag run 1 × 30 yards (inside and outside leg) c. Vertical jump 2 × 8 d. Sprint cutting 4 ×	One-leg quarter squat with medicine ball toss (3 minutes each foot; shoes off)	a. Baby squats 3 × 1 minute (1 squat per second) b. Lateral reach 2 × 10 (perform on each leg)	
11	**Perform dynamic list 5**	Big toe Calves/ankles Quadriceps Hamstrings Hip flexors Iliotibial band (ITB) Hip external rotators Hip internal rotators Shoulders and upper back	a. Box reaction 3 × 30 seconds	Two-knee balance on ball (5 minutes) (If easy, try one knee.)	*Perform the following on each leg:* a. One-leg bridge with hip twist 2 × 30 seconds b. Lateral unders 2 × 15	
12	**Perform dynamic list 6**		a. Depth jumps (from 18-inch height) 2 × 10 b. Tuck jump 2 × 10 c. Ice-skaters 3 × 30 seconds	a. Hop stick landing with back kick (30 yards and back) b. One-foot fire brigade	a. Tether with internal lunge 2 × 30 yards b. Slide board 2 × 30	

(continued)

Level 3 JUMPMETRICS Exercise Progression *(continued)*

DAY	Warm-Up	PT and flex (optional)	Power	Balance	Strength (optional postpractice)	Overload
13	**Perform dynamic list 1**	**Screening exercises** Perform 10 repetitions of the screening exercises you had difficulty with.	a. One-foot twist hop 4 × 15 yards (each leg) 4 × b. One-leg long jump c. Cone pattern 3 × 30 seconds d. Zigzag run 3 × 30 yards (inside and outside leg)	*Perform the following for 1 minute on each foot (shoes off):* a. One-foot balance on balance disc b. Quarter-turn back kick with ground touch	a. Nasty circuit 1 × b. Bench hamstrings with foot on balance disc 2 × 10	**Refer to Level 3 Weekly Strength Program**
14	**Perform dynamic list 2**	*Refer to chapter 2 for explanations of the exercises. Always focus on proper knee position on jumps and landings.*	a. One-foot hop with rotations 2 × 30 yards b. Three-cone reaction 3 × c. Cycle jump 3 × 30 seconds d. Full-spin jump 8 × each way	*Perform the following for 2 minutes on each foot (shoes off):* a. Quarter-turn back kick with ground touch b. Multidirectional kick 2 ×	a. Burpee/squat jump 2 × 10 b. One-leg squat with jump (using hands for support) 3 × 10	
15	**Perform dynamic list 3**	• Single-leg squat • Jumping and landing with good form • Single-leg hops • Bridge	a. Ankle bounce (one foot) 1 × 70 b. One-leg sideways broad jump (15 yards and back) 1 × 12 c. One-leg vertical takeoff d. Called pattern jumps 3 × 30 seconds	*Perform the following for 2 minutes on each foot (shoes off):* a. One-foot balance eyes closed b. Quarter turn with perturbations	a. Slow low step slide with ankle tether (30 yards and back) b. Hip circuit #2	
16	**Perform dynamic list 4**	**Flexibility exercises** *Refer to chapter 2 to perform your assigned flexibility exercises.*	a. Lateral hop 1 × 30 yards b. Zigzag run 1 × 30 yards (inside and outside leg) c. Vertical jump 2 × 8 d. Spring cutting 5 ×	a. Hop stick landing with back kick (30 yards and back) b. Multidirectional kick on balance disc 2 ×	a. Baby squats 3 × 1 minute (1 squat per second) b. One-leg bridge with foot on ball 2 × 30 seconds (perform on each leg)	
17	**Perform dynamic list 5**	Big toe Calves/ankles Quadriceps Hamstrings Hip flexors Iliotibial band (ITB) Hip external rotators Hip internal rotators Shoulders and upper back	Box reaction 3 × 30 seconds	Two-knee balance on ball (5 minutes) (If easy, try on knee.)	a. One-leg bridge with hip twist 2 × 30 seconds (perform on each leg) b. Around the world 1 ×	
18	**Perform dynamic list 6**		a. Depth jumps (from 24-inch height) 2 × 10 b. Tuck jump 2 × 10 c. Ice-skaters 3 × 30 seconds	a. Hop stick landing with back kick (30 yards and back) b. One-foot fire brigade	a. Tether with internal lunge 2 × 30 yards b. Slide boards 2 × 30 +'s	

Level 3 Weekly Strength Program

The level 3 weekly strength program primarily uses external overload resistance exercises. The ability to manage greater and greater resistance during an exercise will significantly affect those muscles and nerves involved during the exercise.

As the resistance becomes greater, it is important to move the weight in a way that helps to develop faster message delivery from your nerves to your muscles—this is referred to as *power*. Production of power (and reactive strength) was discussed in chapter 4. Improving change of direction skills is essential when performing a heavy resistance exercise such as the leg press. The level 3 weekly strength program includes two separate workouts to provide variety and to increase exercise complexity and intensity over time. Each workout is performed over a three-week period to ensure adequate improvements in muscular strength and power.

To enhance power, you should never push to complete exhaustion when you begin using an exercise. Going to a point where the muscle is too exhausted to allow movement, also called momentary muscular failure (MMF), is counterproductive to long-term power production. Increases in power are created by the ability of your body to send rapid nerve messages. Exhaustive work is often performed with slow and continuous movement patterns. The production of power requires heavy loads that are moved quickly from the stretch portion of the movement into the contraction or muscle-shortening segment of the movement. Repeated bouts of MMF deplete levels of neurotransmitters, which reduces nerve efficiency. Going to MMF may be a good way to build the size of the muscle tissue because the muscle is placed under greater stress in the absence of energy-saving momentum. However, over time it will reduce the ability of the nerves to perform at their highest level. The resistance during the first exposure to any exercise should be light to moderate. This means you should easily complete all of the assigned repetitions in the first two sets, and complete all of the repetitions in the last set as well, but your muscles should feel like they have done something when you have finished the exercise. As the weeks pass, the resistance should increase slowly over the workout sets to a point where you are barely able to complete the final repetition on the final workout of the plan. Finding your starting weight is the difficult part, so you should begin with very light resistance. It is easier to constructively work your way upward in resistance, rather than experiencing MMF too soon and taking the chance of reducing the effectiveness of the workout plan. Concentrate on increasing the resistance on the final set of each exercise over the length of the level 3 program (see table 10.1). The level 3 workouts are performed on weeks 9 through 14 of the total Jumpmetrics plan.

TABLE 10.1

Example of Resistance Progression in the Leg Press

Week	Day 1	Day 2	Day 3
9	6 × 120	6 × 130	6 × 150
10	6 × 120	6 × 130	6 × 160
11	6 × 120	6 × 140	6 × 165
12	5 × 130	5 × 150	5 × 175
13	5 × 130	5 × 150	5 × 185
14	5 × 130	5 × 160	5 × 190

JUMPMETRICS

Level 3 Weekly Strength Program

WEEKS 9-11

Monday

Leg press	6 × ___	6 × ___	6 × ___
Baby squats		1 minute	1 minute
Hip circuit #2			1 ×
Bench hamstrings	10 × ___	10 × ___	8 × ___
Calf raise leg press		25 × ___	25 × ___
Cylinder circuit #1			1 ×

Wednesday

Bench press	6 × ___	6 × ___	6 × ___
Push press		6 × ___	6 × ___
Power pull		8 × ___	8 × ___
Hammer curl (walking rack)		5 × 4 drops in weight	
Runner's rear deltoid		30 seconds	30 seconds
Cylinder circuit #2			1 ×

Friday

Squat	6 × ___	6 × ___	6 × ___
One-leg squat	8 × ___	8 × ___	8 × ___
Leg extension		10 × ___	10 × ___
Leg curl	8 × ___	8 × ___	8 × ___
One-leg bridge with foot on big ball		30 seconds	30 seconds
Cylinder circuit #3			1 ×

▶ You must increase weight with each set where resistance is used. The last set is the power set and must increase in weight each week (therefore, do not start too heavy). Increase repetitions where body weight or a weighted vest is used.

JUMPMETRICS

Level 3 Weekly Strength Program

Monday

Squat	5 × ___	5 × ___	5 × ___
One-leg squat (weight vest)	8 × ___	8 × ___	8 × ___
Around the world			2 ×
Runner's leg curl	8 × ___	8 × ___	8 × ___
Calf raise leg press		25 × ___	25 × ___
Cylinder circuit #1			1 ×

Wednesday

Hang clean with jerk	5 × ___	5 × ___
Dumbbell split snatch	5 × ___	5 × ___
Leg drag	15 yards and back	15 yards and back
French press	5 × ___	5 × ___
Hammer curl	6 × ___	6 × ___
Cylinder circuit #2		1 ×

Friday

Leg press	5 × ___	5 × ___	5 × ___
Pull-ups		10 × ___	10 × ___
(Add 3 negatives if 10 is not obtained.)			
Dumbbell push press		5 × ___	5 × ___
Bench hamstrings (weight vest)	10 × ___	10 × ___	8 × ___
One-leg bridge with foot on big ball		30 seconds	30 seconds)
Cylinder circuit #3			1 ×

▶ You must increase weight with each set where resistance is used. The last set is the power set and must increase in weight each week (therefore, do not start too heavy). Increase repetitions where body weight or a weighted vest is used.

About the Authors

Alan Tyson, PT, SCS, ATC-L, CSCS, is a licensed physical therapist, a certified athletic trainer and a certified strength and conditioning specialist. He is the director of Physical Therapy at Carolinas Physical Therapy Network. He has worked two years with the Charlotte Knights and continues to serve as a consultant to the team. Tyson is also a consultant with the Carolina Panthers. He has been treating biomechanical issues of pitcher's shoulder and elbow for the past eight years and is developing an injury database with Davidson College and the University of North Carolina at Charlotte.

Ben Cook, MA, CSCS, NSCA-CPT, is currently the manager of sports performance at the Epicenter Sports Performance Enhancement Center. Ben has worked with high school, college, and professional athletes in strength and conditioning for 18 years. From 1993-2001 he was the Strength and Conditioning Coach for men's basketball at the University of North Carolina at Chapel Hill. Ben earned his master's degree in Exercise and Sports Science from the University of North Carolina and is a certified personal trainer and strength and conditioning specialist.

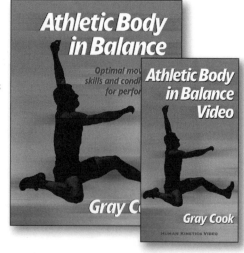

2335